# in the GLOW of the SIERRA

## GHOST TOWNS & HISTORICAL SITES OF THE EASTERN SIERRA: SOUTHERN REGION

Editing and Publishing Services provided by Stacey Smekofske, Edits by Stacey
Proofreading by Jo Johnston
Map illustrations by Austin Metz
Book design by Tara Mayberry, TeaBerryStudio.com

ISBN: Hardcover: 979-8-9992388-3-2
       Paperback: 979-8-9992388-4-9
       eBook: 979-8-9992388-5-6

*To Nancy Force*

*Thank you for passing on a love of travel.*

*You taught me to always be on, or planning a trip,*

*and how to be a strong and independent woman.*

*"Traveling—it leaves you speechless,*
*then turns you into a storyteller."*

*—Ibn Battuta*

# CONTENTS

# ACKNOWLEDGMENTS

Many people deserve thanks for making *In the Glow of the Sierra* a reality.

In 2020, I decided my midlife goal was to visit and photograph every ghost town in Nevada and the Eastern Sierra. I had no idea where it would take me!

> **In 2020, I decided my midlife goal was to visit and photograph every ghost town in Nevada and the Eastern Sierra. I had no idea where it would take me!**

I started amassing vast amounts of photos and talked with my longest-term friend, Tara Mayberry, a book designer and owner of TeaBerry Creative. A book was in my mind, but it was too large a project to undertake. With Tara's advice and help, I started a blog and social media. Neither of us realized Nevada Ghost Towns & Beyond would become my full-time job. Five years later, the book I dreamed of became a reality. There was never any doubt Tara would design it. She is the one to thank for the beautiful design, layout, and for supporting me through the process.

When my first book was a seed in my mind, amazing local historians, authors, and photographers, Karen Dustman and Judy Wickwire, asked me to breakfast. Even though I had met both, it felt like they had a goal in mind. The reason for the meeting came out at the end of breakfast: they wanted to know when I was writing my first book.

Still debating which book idea to pursue first, I took my good friend Mike on a day exploring the Carson River Route. We ended with lunch in Markleeville in the 1862 Fiske House relocated from the ghost town of Silver Mountain City. I weighed out all the options in excruciating detail. In his usual direct style, Mike told me to shut up and do it.

I have met many wonderful people over the years of exploring ghost towns. Many trusted me with sites, knowing I would respect them and uncover their buried history. Thank you to Rick, Jared, and others who took me to lesser-known locations.

When I started exploring, I would take our town SUV or BNT, the Big Noisy Truck. It soon became apparent I needed a more capable off-road vehicle. Steve lives not far from me, but we met online when I was debating vehicle options. Deciding a Jeep was the best for me, Steve searched for the right Rubicon. After I got my Jeep, Honey Badger, he walked me through modifications and repaired the damage she received on my explorations. We became good friends and have taken numerous trips around Nevada and the Eastern Sierra. Steve and his amazing wife, Patty, have become like an extended family. A geologist, ghost town enthusiast, emigrant trail, and train lover, Steve reviewed the book for its technical terminology and historical facts.

Years ago, I came across the website *Nevada Expeditions*. After I started my site, I reached out to the creator, Austin Metz, and told him how much I enjoyed his work. Austin became my primary exploring partner. While we are from different backgrounds, sometimes it feels like we are the same person. Our friendship has grown beyond ghost towns, and he has supported me through life and the book. I half-joke that if we were teenage girls, I would buy us a heart-shaped split "best friend" necklace. He went above and beyond reviewing the book for historical correctness and grammar.

When I built my website, I thought if you built it, they would come. I quickly learned that wasn't the case, so I started social media accounts. I remember how excited I was when I reached 600 followers. Sliding into 20,000, I have the best readers. I genuinely enjoy interacting with them; they have encouraged and pushed me to stretch my explorations and research. Thank you to all my loyal followers.

Along my travels, I expanded my training. Through various groups, I learned off-roading skills, repairs, and recovery techniques.

A special thank you to Clint and Heidi Smith, Jack Daniel, and the other instructors at Thunder Ranch. If I'm not on the trail or researching, Thunder Ranch is my other happy place. Over multiple classes, I learned about self-protection and emergency medical treatment.

Stanley Paher started my journey to Nevada's ghost towns. Explorers consider his book, *Nevada Ghost Towns & Mining Camps*, the bible of ghost towns. I met Stan a few times over the years. He became a mentor, friend, and a great companion on exploring and camping trips. Stan encouraged me to publish this book, telling me this was the first of many. A very special thank you, Stan, for reviewing sections for historical correctness.

Thank you to all of my beta readers. Your feedback significantly improved the book and motivated me to reach the finish line. A special thank you to authors and historians Jeanne Sharp-Howerton and Karen Dustman, who not only edited but also acted as my emotional support authors.

Thank you to my excellent editor, Stacey Smekofske. Tara recommended her, saying she was the best. During our first meeting, I discovered that she was from Nevada, lived not far from where I grew up in Idaho, and loved the desert. Stacey made the process as easy as possible by editing and assisting with the publication. She won my heart when I told her I couldn't reach one site due to washouts. We both loved the story, as it involved several locations, and we found a way to incorporate them.

I convinced my mom and dad to take me to my first ghost town, Silver City, Idaho. My dad gave me my love for the outdoors and taking the back road. While my mom might not understand my need to be in the middle of nowhere, she is the first one to support and cheer me on. In the summers while growing up, she was always traveling the west coast, with us in tow.

My family has been my biggest supporter. After I decided to start a website, we discussed at dinner how I would approach it as a regular job and see where it went. They have been there every step of the way, encouraging and supporting me. My son is a history lover and finds interesting stories for me to research. My daughter is my mini-me and always makes sure I take care of myself. Hubby ensures I have everything I might need while on my travels. They hold down the fort when I'm gone, put up with the trips and my incessant talk about ghost towns.

*Thank you all!*

# A NOTE TO THE READERS

At fourteen and a half, I got my driver's license and first car. It's an Idaho thing and seemed like a grand idea to teenage me. Even at an early age, I knew vehicles were magical, a combination of freedom and exploration.

In 2000, I married a third-generation Nevada ranch boy. He wanted to see more of the Silver State on our first vacation. Instead of the usual tourist guides, I purchased Stanley Paher's *Nevada Ghost Towns and Mining Camps*. Using it as a guide, I planned a week-long ghost town adventure. As our family grew, we spent our vacations exploring the Nevada desert and Eastern Sierra ghost towns.

I raised my family and ran a business, focusing on others. As the family became more independent, my husband told me this was my time to focus on myself. I was at a loss for how to fill my time. One evening, I announced to the family that my mid-life goal was to photograph every ghost town in Nevada and the Eastern Sierra. Little did I know where it would lead me.

I was an anomaly compared to the other women my age. They purchased sports cars, took dance classes, and headed to the wine country. I bought a Rubicon and pointed it toward the desert. I learned off-roading, recovery skills, wilderness first aid, and self-protection. I traded dress clothes and heels for tactical pants and packer boots.

My Jeep, Honey Badger, is a 2013, 10th-anniversary Rubicon. She earned her name because she does not care what our travels throw at her. Despite everything, she keeps going, just like me.

For five years, I explored ghost towns and historic sites, documenting their history and my travels through my website, *Nevada Ghost Towns & Beyond*, NVTami on social media, presentations at museums and historical societies, articles in *Nevada Magazine* and a show on KGFN, Radio Goldfield, the "Voice of the Old West."

> **I hope you enjoy the photos and history and love the Eastern Sierra as much as I do. While it is in the glow of the Sierra, nothing out shines its history and beauty.**

*In the Glow of the Sierra* is a compilation of my travels along the southern region of the Eastern Sierra. The book covers the 270-mile range from Mono County in the north to Kern County in the south.

I hope you enjoy the photos and history and love the Eastern Sierra as much as I do. While it is in the shadow of the Sierra, nothing overshadows its history and beauty.

# INTRODUCTION

Dividing Eastern California from the west coast, the Sierra stretches four hundred miles from Lassen County to the corner of Kern County. The range isolates Eastern California from the rest of the state and creates a dichotomy between the slopes.

The northern end of the range is in the Sierra rain shadow. Snow-covered peaks give way to ragged hills, which in turn lead to the desert. The snow-melt creates an environment that is productive for ranching. Early pioneers settled the land to provide meat, produce, and livestock for emigrants on the California Trail. A decade later, they fed the famed Comstock Lode and Bodie boom.

**The Southern Sierra region is home to towering peaks, including Mount Whitney, the tallest peak in the contiguous United States, and glaciers that cut a swath of ragged peaks, deep canyons, and U-shaped valleys.**

The Southern Sierra region is distinct from the Northern Sierra region. It is home to towering peaks, including the 14,505 ft Mount Whitney, the tallest peak in the contiguous United States. Glaciers cut a swath of ragged peaks, deep canyons, and U-shaped valleys. The precipitous slope abruptly transitions from the high peaks to the valleys below. Due to the proximity to the Sierra rain shadow effect, the southern end of the range receives less rainfall, resulting in an arid climate.

John Muir, famed naturalist and "Father of the National Parks," lived in the Sierra from 1868 to 1874. He named the Sierra "The range of light" after witnessing how the sunlight played with the granite peaks, valleys, and meadows, creating a heavenly glow.

Indigenous tribes, including the Paiute and Shoshone, have long inhabited the Eastern Sierra. They often moved seasonally, leaving few permanent traces.

Between 1829 and 1848, early emigrants to California followed the Spanish Trail—the 2,700-mile route connected Santa Fe, New Mexico, and Los Angeles, California. Due to mountain passes, deserts, and deep canyons, the Spanish Trail was one of the most challenging trade routes in US history. Few settled in the inhospitable southeastern Sierra.

In 1857, German prospector Cord Norst and his wife, set up camp on Virginia Creek, ninety miles south of Genoa, Utah Territory. They built a dugout house with rock walls on the hillside and panned gold for a living. Word of their discoveries spread, and prospectors flocked to the area, looking to stake their claim. Eventually, they set up dwellings; some had tents, but many used what was available, building shelters of rocks or even holes in the ground covered in branches. Dog Town was the first settlement, followed by Monoville, which was the first official "town" of the Eastern Sierra, south of Genoa.

Prospectors expanded their search, panning creeks for gold and scouting for float, fragments of ore shed from a rock outcropping, often quartz. With the discovery of a promising ledge, mining camps sprang to life.

Saloon owners set up businesses, followed by brothels, which were often operated out of wagons and tents. Developers arrived, dividing parcels, planning towns, and selling land they did not own. Soon, a town sprang to life. Stores, assay offices, boarding houses, and restaurants opened. Schoolhouses and churches created legitimacy and permanence, and fortunate settlements gained a post office.

Bodie brought the Eastern Sierra international focus. W.S. Bodey (or Body) discovered gold in 1859, but the rush was almost two decades later, in 1876–1877. Within a handful of years, Bodie had a population of between 7,000 and 10,000, with nearly every service imaginable. Bodie's mines produced an estimated $38 million in gold (over $1 billion in 2025).

Along the Eastern Sierra, other towns followed suit, but few with the same magnitude as Bodie. Only one town, Cerro Gordo, came close to Bodie's boom.

Mining gold, silver, and other minerals required immense infrastructure with an insatiable need for lumber, fuel, and building supplies. Lumber yards, charcoal and lime kilns dotted the region.

In Mono Basin and Owens Valley, settlers developed farms and ranches to feed the growing populations of the mining towns.

States and local entities awarded toll road franchises to individuals or groups who bid to construct and maintain roads. In return for their investment, travelers compensated the owners with tolls.

In 1867, the Central Pacific Railroad reached the Eastern Sierra at Reno, Nevada. In 1872, the Virginia & Truckee Railroad (V&T) connected the Comstock mines to the world. Almost a decade later, in 1880, the Carson & Colorado Railroad left the V&T at Mound House, Nevada. Within three years, it extended to Keeler and the famous Cerro Gordo mines. Steam locomotives required water, resulting in water stops that sprang to life every seven to ten miles. Settlements developed around the water towers to offer travelers a respite from their journey.

Eventually, the mines played out. This could happen within weeks, years, or sometimes decades. With little tying people to the area, most moved on, often farther east, to the mining boom around Goldfield and Rhyolite, Nevada. Towns were soon abandoned, joining the growing list of ghost towns. Residents took what they could carry, and they abandoned everything else, including possessions and houses.

Those who lost their lives in the pursuit of riches were often the only ones who remained to mark the boom period. Headstones mark some graves, but many are only mounds covered in rocks with any marker of their life lost to the ravages of time.

The harsh Eastern Sierra challenged miners and settlers, but it also protected the remains of their time in isolated locations. History dots the Eastern Sierra. Ghost towns, mines and mills, abandoned ranches... all in the glow of the Sierra.

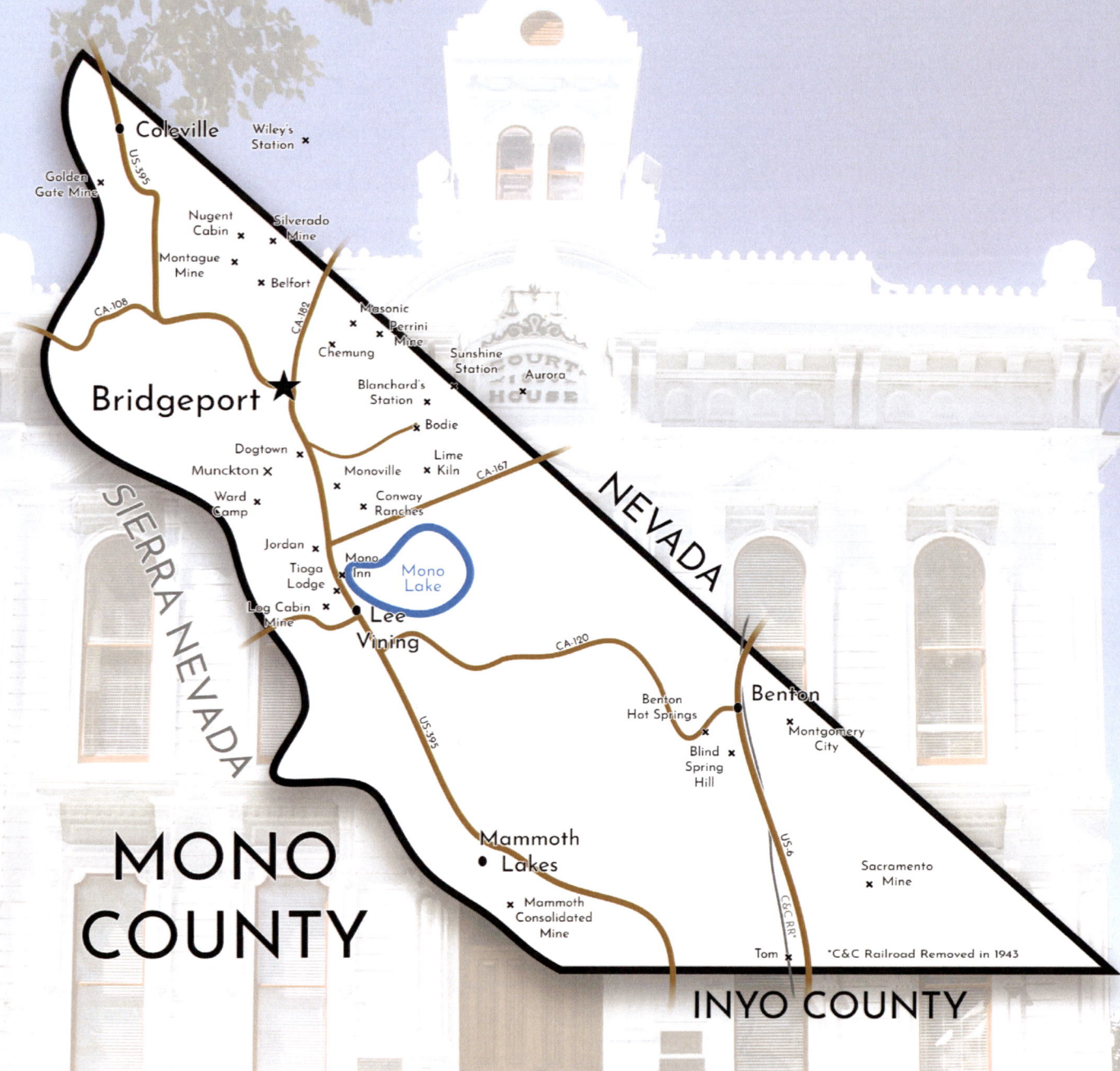

Coleville

Wiley's Station

Golden Gate Mine

US-395

Nugent Cabin

Silverado Mine

Montague Mine

Belfort

CA-108

CA-182

Masonic
Perrini Mine

Chemung

Sunshine Station

Aurora

Bridgeport

Blanchard's Station

Bodie

Dogtown

Lime Kiln

Munckton

Monoville

CA-167

Ward Camp

Conway Ranches

Jordan

Mono Inn

Mono Lake

Tioga Lodge

Log Cabin Mine

Lee Vining

CA-120

Benton Hot Springs

Benton

Montgomery City

Blind Spring Hill

US-395

US-6

Mammoth Lakes

Sacramento Mine

Mammoth Consolidated Mine

C&C RR*

*C&C Railroad Removed in 1943

Tom

SIERRA NEVADA

NEVADA

MONO COUNTY

INYO COUNTY

# *Chapter One*: MONO COUNTY

## The Mono tribe was the first to call what is now Mono County home. The Eastern Mono, or Owens Valley Paiute, is the southernmost tribe of the Northern Paiutes in the Eastern Sierra.

In 1844, the Frémont Party crossed the Sierra. Frémont was known as "The Great Pathfinder." Along with his guide, Kit Carson, his battalion expanded western overland exploration, opening the American West. After exploring the Eastern Sierra, the party crossed the range before winter from the Bridgeport area. Snowstorms hampered efforts, and the party abandoned an 1836 mountain howitzer in a canyon.

While pursuing Chief Teneiya and members of the Ahwahneechee Tribe, Lt. Tredwell Moore arrived in the Mono Basin in 1852. He failed to capture the chief but discovered gold-bearing quartz and other minerals. The samples were displayed in San Francisco, generating interest from the mining community. By fall, Leroy Vining and others settled the basin to search for gold.

In 1857, German prospector Cord Norst and his wife, Mary, a Native American, set up camp on a creek north of Mono Lake. They built a dugout house with rock walls on the hillside and panned gold for a living. Hearing of their discovery, Mormons from Genoa headed south to stake claims along the creeks. Dog Town soon became a "bustling community" of one hundred miners.

Prospectors expanded their search for gold and silver, and soon, most residents of Dog Town relocated to Monoville. In 1860, silver was discovered fifteen miles north, and the town of Aurora exploded overnight.

Ranchers and farmers tamed the land and diverted water to provide beef and produce for the mining camps. In 1861, the California Legislature created Mono County, one of four counties in the Eastern Sierra. The land included portions of Calaveras, Fresno, and Mariposa counties. In 1864, a portion of Mono County became Alpine County, and in 1866, the southern portion created Inyo County.

Aurora was the first seat of Mono County, California. Bridgeport assumed this honor in 1863 after a survey determined Aurora was in Nevada. In 1880, the county constructed a beautiful Italianate-style courthouse.

Though Bodie was discovered as early as 1859, it struggled to survive for two decades. In 1877, Bodie boomed with the discovery of rich, gold-bearing ore. The town grew to a population of 10,000. By the end of the century, the glory was short-lived. Bodie and the other mining towns faded as miners moved to more promising prospects.

Mono County returned to a slower pace of life; ranching and tourism kept its towns alive. Today, Mono County is a four-season tourist mecca: skiing and snowboarding in the winter, hiking and fishing in summer, and leaf peeping in the fall.

# GOLDEN GATE MINE

In 1898, miners discovered mineral-bearing quartz veins at the Eastern Sierra's foot and struck a claim. The mine expanded in 1900 when owners discovered a quartz lode they proclaimed was "a producer of great merit." Miners dug and blasted drifts as long as 1,800 feet into the solid rock. They transported ore to the mill with a 2,300-foot aerial tramway. Mercury was then used to extract gold from the ore.

The Eastern Sierra is prone to heavy snow. In 1907, an avalanche destroyed the mill and other buildings. The miners rebuilt 200 feet from the site at the foot of a hill they thought was safe. In March 1911, another avalanche destroyed the bunkhouse, stable, and water intake. No one died, and miners sustained only minor injuries. A week later, a third avalanche destroyed the boarding house. Owners rebuilt, including a ten-stamp mill and a large boarding house.

Golden Gate was the sole remaining stamp mill on public lands in the region. The Bureau of Land Management and the National Park Service stabilized the 113-year-old stamp mill in 2005. On August 29, 2020, lightning strikes caused a fire in nearby Slinkard Valley. The Slink Fire burned out of control despite extensive fire suppression efforts. The historic structures were in a narrow, heavily wooded canyon and rapidly consumed by flames.

# WILEY'S STATION

Robert and Margaret Wiley emigrated west in 1864. They operated several hotels and stage stops, including Nine Mile Ranch. Wiley's Station was a stage stop on the Carson-Aurora stage line from the 1860s through the 1870s.

Wiley's Station is in beautiful Dalzell Canyon, a narrow valley between the Pine Grove Hills and the Sweetwater Mountains. The California border runs through the canyon, leaving the flats just over the Nevada border.

# NUGENT CABIN

The Nugent Cabin was a line cabin for ranchers. Over the years, several families and off-road groups have loved and cared for it well. It is open to whoever wants to stay there on a first-come basis. The rule is to leave it better than you found it. People have replaced windows and decorated, cleaned, and stocked the cabin.

A collapsed log cabin nearby indicates that miners may have used the site in the 1860s.

# BELFORT &
# BOULDER FLAT

Miners were drawn to the Sweetwater Range in the 1860s to harvest trees for use in the mines and towns of Aurora and Pine Grove. While cutting lumber, prospectors explored the area and found promising mining locations. Half a dozen mining towns sprang up in the Sweetwater Range.

Mining was productive enough to form the Patterson Mining District in the 1880s. The most active years of the district were between 1882 and 1883, with a value of $500,000 ($15 million in 2025) produced between 1880 and 1884. Ore veins ran out within ten years, and by 1888, only one mine in the Patterson District remained active. By 1890, miners abandoned Star City. They dismantled structures to relocate to new strikes. The Patterson District saw some mining activity in the early 1900s, but Belfort, Boulder Flat, and Star City remained ghost towns.

# SILVERADO MINE

Miners first worked the Silverado Mine in Silverado Canyon in the 1860s. It was a major producer of high-grade silver. The mine included a steam-powered ten-stamp mill, and mules transported ore to the mill.

In 1891, A.P. Sayer discovered a rich strike running from Silverado Canyon. Sayer was well respected in the Patterson Mining District, and the *Mono Herald* and *Bridgeport Chronicle Union* reported, "There is no one in the district more deserving as he has done much hard work in it."

In 1917, thirty men worked at Silverado. Owners added a fifty-ton mill. Shipping was through Hudson on the Nevada Copper Belt Railroad. The mine went through multiple cycles of activity and inactivity into the 1950s.

When you think about miners, the last thing you might imagine is a gift for verse. Yet Tom Burke was a budding poet. In his spare time at Silverado, he wrote in rhyme about leaving the comfort of town to search for gold. You can find a sample in *Mono Herald and Bridgeport Chronicle Union,* January 5, 1918.

BUCKWHEAT GROWING BY THE CABIN

# MONTAGUE MINE & MT. PATTERSON STONE CABIN

D ue to its elevation of 10,961 feet, miners could only work the Montague Mine between July and October, which is when winter storms moved in. The Montague Mine was an underground mine that primarily produced gold and some silver. It is in the Comstock Gold-Silver Belt, which runs on the crest of the Sweetwater Range.

The stone cabin sits perched on the side of the desolate Mt. Patterson, which is nick-named "Mars with flowers" due to its likeness to the red planet.

According to a man who helped stabilize the cabin, Guy Montague owned the mine. He had previously worked in the Balatoc gold mine in the Philippines and built the cabin between 1937 and 1939. Order L-208 closed non-war-related mining during World War II. Due to the low grade of silver, it was not reopened following the war, as with many of the great gold and silver mines of the West.

# MASONIC

In 1860, Freemasons found gold ten miles northeast of Bridgeport. They named the area Masonic after their order. More significant regional strikes drew them away, and the claims remained undeveloped. In 1900, sixteen-year-old Joe Green from nearby Bodie rediscovered Masonic and founded the Jump Up Joe Mine. He had no capital to work the mine, so he sold the claim.

On July 4, 1902, partners John Stuart Phillips, Caleb Dorsey, and John M. Bryan struck gold. They named their mine the Pittsburg-Liberty Mine in honor of Phillips's hometown and its discovery on Independence Day. At that time, *Pittsburg,* Pennsylvania, was not spelled with an "H."

Initially, Masonic consisted of three separate towns: Upper Town, Middle Town, and Lower Town. The three towns eventually combined under the single name Masonic. Unlike many towns at the time, there were no churches, fraternal groups, or brothels. Ironically, there was never a Masonic Lodge in Masonic.

In contrast to the reputations of nearby Bodie and Aurora, Masonic was known for being a law-abiding, peaceful town.

Upper Town, originally Lorena, had mine offices, and a post office opened in 1905. The post office name was officially changed to Masonic in 1906.

Middle Town held a hotel, store, stage station, school, and post office.

Lower town was previously named Calivada. In 1907, the Pittsburg-Liberty Mill opened a ten-stamp mill in Lower Town. The mine constructed an aerial tramway to transport ore from the mines to the mill.

In 1909, Pittsburg-Liberty Mine owner, John Phillips fell to his death in a mine shaft. It is not known if this was an accident or murder. Soon after, the ore vanished. The mine sold multiple times, but the pockets of gold were exhausted. The post office closed in 1927. Sporadic attempts at mining were made from the 1950s to 1960s with limited success.

PITTSBURG-LIBERTY MILL

AERIAL TRAMWAY

# PERRINI MINE

Bodie Hills is twelve miles northeast of Bridgeport and sixteen miles northwest of Bodie. The district bordered Nevada, so Esmeralda County, Nevada, registered some Masonic District claims despite them being in California.

The peak of mining activity in the Masonic District occurred between 1906 and 1911. After that, production was sporadic due to uneven ore deposits and the processing required. Limited mining continued into the 1930s, but the veins were shallow, and miners only developed shafts a few hundred feet deep. Between 1930 and 1960, production was so sparse that the district did not record it.

The Perrini Mine is outside of the Masonic District, just inside the California border. It was a gold mine in the early 1900s.

# CHEMUNG MINE & MILL

In 1900, Stephen Kavanaugh was hired to excavate a gold vein along a ridge two and a half miles southwest of Masonic. The site overlooks Bridgeport Valley from an 8,600-foot mountain perch. Stephen established the Chemung Mine in 1909, naming it after his hometown of Chemung, Illinois. As Stephen was an employee, he did not receive a share of the mine's profits.

Chemung was a productive gold and silver mine but was overshadowed by nearby Bodie. Nevertheless, in twenty-nine years of operation, Chemung produced over $1 million in gold ($34 million in 2025). The ore was processed on site and then shipped to Bodie for smelting.

Chemung consisted of a mill, mine offices, a bunkhouse, and a general store. Multiple legal issues related to land ownership and the mine lease, caused the mill to be torn down and rebuilt three times.

Legend says the mill's owner fell, or maybe was pushed, down a mine shaft. Some say his spirit still haunts Chemung, but in a twist, only on Saturday nights.

# BRIDGEPORT

Ranchers settled in Bridgeport Valley, known as "Big Meadows," in 1859. Prospectors had to ford the East Walker River to access the mining camps. Businessmen took advantage and created a "port" with stores, restaurants, and livery services. Initially known as "Port with a Ford," then "Port with a Bridge," the town simplified the name to Bridgeport.

Aurora was the first seat of Mono County. Following the Sagebrush War in Susanville and a survey of California's eastern border, surveyors found in 1863 that Aurora was in Nevada, not California. In 1864, the county moved the seat to the small town of Bridgeport. The town was so small it didn't have a post office until the year it became the county seat.

The county built a beautiful Italianate-style courthouse in 1880. It is still in use and is California's second oldest continuously used courthouse.

# AURORA, NEVADA

In 1860, a trio of miners discovered ore near the Nevada/California border, and the town of Aurora was born. Within a year, 1,400 people called Aurora home. The town included almost 800 homes, twenty stores, and twenty-two saloons.

Aurora was the epitome of the Wild West. Men slung pistols on their hips, and conflict often resulted in gunfights. Entertainment included saloons, brothels, and dog- vs. badger-fights. Half the women in town were prostitutes, many from China. Samuel Clemens, later known by his pen-name Mark Twain, lived and mined in Aurora from spring to fall of 1862.

Aurora has a unique distinction: it was simultaneously the seat of two counties. When California became a state in 1850, the 120-degree west longitude was its eastern border. On six occasions from 1855 to 1900, surveys attempted to locate the 120-degree longitude, each with different results—the boundary discrepancy led to multiple issues. In Aurora, the town was the seat of Esmeralda County, Nevada, and Mono County, California. On Election Day, residents voted for Esmeralda County and then walked to the next polling station to vote for Mono County. In 1863, Aurora lost the Mono County seat when it was officially determined to be in Nevada.

Aurora faded as quickly as it boomed. By 1864, half of the town's seventeen mills had ceased operations, and six years later, half of the houses had been abandoned.

Aurora experienced several revivals, including the 1870s, with mining in Bodie. In 1883, the town, once the seat of two counties, lost the Esmeralda County seat to Hawthorne; the post office closed in 1897. Aurora experienced a final revival in the early 1900s with an uptick in mining. The post office reopened in 1906, and electrical power arrived in 1910. This cycle lasted a decade. In 1918, the school closed, followed by the post office the following year.

SUNSHINE STATION

BLANCHARD STATION

# SUNSHINE & BLANCHARD'S STATIONS

In 1862, nine miners were awarded a franchise to develop a toll road connecting Bodie to Aurora and eventually to Genoa. The road wound through the narrow Bodie Gulch, where, in places, sheer rock walls soar to the sky, allowing in only a sliver of sunlight.

Between the 1880s and 1890s, Hank Blanchard operated a portion of the toll road. Blanchard's Station was midway between Bodie and the state line. Sunshine Station sat just inside Nevada, halfway between the two towns, earning it the alternate name Halfway House. Two to three stages ran daily in each direction.

Stagecoach robberies were common in Bodie Canyon. Sharp curves, narrow passages, steep cliffs, and isolation were ideal for a ne'er-do-well looking to enhance his income. It is said that robberies occurred so often that horse teams would halt themselves in the canyon to await arriving highwaymen.

Stories differ on how stagecoach robbers behaved. Some robbers were polite, not touching passengers or their belongings. Other hold-ups were at gunpoint, where robbers demanded passengers place all their valuables in the bandit's hat or sack. After freeing the passengers from their possessions, the highwaymen made a fast, clean getaway. One agreeable highwayman posed for a photograph during a robbery, taking an 1880s-style selfie with his victims!

BLANCHARD STATION

# BODIE

When people think of ghost towns, Bodie often comes to mind. How can it not? It is likely the most famous ghost town—visitors from across the world trek across the Sierra to walk the streets and peek into abandoned buildings. Since Bodie became a state park in 1962, the town has been in a state of "arrested decay," freezing it in time.

Bodie started as an unassuming mining camp following the discovery of gold by W.S. Bodey in 1859. Tragically, Bodey froze to death in a winter storm while trying to reach Monoville for supplies, and the town was named in his honor. While nearby Aurora boomed, Bodie remained a small camp. By 1868, the town's two-stamp mills ceased activity.

The Standard Company found gold in 1876. Within a few years, Bodie boomed and boasted a population of 10,000. Services rivaled big cities: banks, unions, newspapers, a railroad, and even a brass band. Nine stamp mills were in operation, shipping bullion to the mint in Carson City, Nevada.

Bodie's mines started to decline in 1879. By 1886, the population was only 1,500. In July 1892, a fire destroyed much of the downtown. Residents rebuilt, but on a smaller scale. By 1920, only 120 people remained at Bodie. In 1932, young William "Bodie Bill" Brewster played with matches behind the Old Sawdust Saloon, and that fire quickly grew, destroying much of Main Street.

Mines continued to operate until the start of World War II when the US War Production Board issued Order L-208, which halted all mining that did not support the war effort. Bodie's post office closed in 1942.

# DOG TOWN

In 1857, German prospector Cord Norst and his wife, Mary, a Native American, set up camp on Virginia Creek. They built a dugout house with rock walls on the hillside and panned gold for a living.

Hearing of their discovery, Mormons from Genoa headed south to stake claims along Virginia and Dog Creeks. Dog Town soon became a "bustling community" of one hundred miners.

On July 4, 1859, a town resident left the Independence Day festivities and wandered the hills east of Dog Town. He rested, picked up some dirt, and found it contained gold. Most Dog Town residents relocated and created the new town of Monoville before anyone else could stake claims.

The Norst couple chose to remain at Dog Town. They homesteaded land and continued to pan for gold, purchasing supplies in the new town of Bridgeport.

It is unknown how much Dog Town produced; it is thought that, along with Monoville, the miners extracted several million dollars in gold. While production is minor compared to Bodie, if it weren't for Dog Town, Bodie might have never existed.

The name Dog Town might sound unique and quirky, but it was a fairly common name in the Old West. There are two stories about the origin of the name. First, Dog Town is a name miners gave to a location with miserable living conditions where they lived like dogs.

The second theory is more literal. A woman moved to town with three dogs. Dogs did what dogs do and got busy. The male miners were lonely and happy to buy a puppy. Before too long, canines overran Dog Town.

DOG TOWN
1857

SITE OF THE FIRST MAJOR GOLD RUSH TO CALIFORNIA'S
EASTERN SLOPE OF THE SIERRA NEVADA, DOG TOWN
DERIVED ITS NAME FROM A POPULAR MINERS' TERM
FOR CAMPS WITH HUTS OR HOVELS. RUINS, LYING
CLOSE TO THE CLIFF BORDERING DOG TOWN CREEK,
ARE ALL THAT REMAIN OF THE MAKESHIFT DWELLINGS
WHICH HERE FORMED PART OF THE "DIGGINS."

CALIFORNIA REGISTERED HISTORICAL LANDMARK NO. 792

PLAQUE PLACED BY THE CALIFORNIA STATE PARK
COMMISSION IN COOPERATION WITH THE MONO COUNTY
DEPARTMENT OF PARKS AND RECREATION AND THE
MONO COUNTY HISTORICAL SOCIETY SEPTEMBER 11, 1964.

# MUNCKTON

In 1867, Charles Snyder explored Dog Town Creek to locate the source of a placer gold nugget. The nugget was the largest discovered on the eastern slope of the Sierra, fourteen miles west of Bodie. He found quartz veins on Kavanaugh Ridge, dug a forty-foot tunnel, and transported three tons of ore to Aurora for processing. He named his mine Dunderberg, possibly after the Union warship the USS *Dunderberg*. While his payout was only $150 ($3,300 in 2025), it was enough for him to continue working on the claim. In June of the same year, Snyder established the Castle Peak Mining District to protect his claim.

Word of Snyder's find spread, and soon, miners staked additional claims. Druggist Dr. George Munckton founded the Munckton Gold and Silver Mining Company. Munckton made his money with a large strike at Aurora and sought a subsequent big claim. He purchased the Dunderberg Mine from Snyder. The settlement continued to grow, and the town became known as Munckton. The town contained saloons, general stores, an assay office, a livery, a boarding house, and, of course, a drug store. A post office opened in 1871.

Due to high sulfide levels, processing ore was complex, and soon, the mill ceased operation. Miners and merchants moved on to more prosperous mines, and the post office closed in 1872.

DUNDERBERG MILL

# WARD MINING CAMP

While Munckton was suffering multiple issues, miners explored the area around the town. They discovered promising ore around Green Creek and located mining claims, including Castle Peak, Ironside, and Bulkhead.

Thomas Ward developed a small settlement and constructed a water-powered four-stamp mill in 1892. The mill processed ore from local claims. Eight years later, the property and stamp mill came under the ownership of H.P. Hayes and Steve Kavanaugh.

The Ward Mine and Mill changed hands frequently. The last known owner of Ward was Ed L. Page. Ed had legs that were crippled, and he created crutches from branches. He hobbled between the stamp mill and Ward Mine, over 2,000 feet, primarily vertically. He continued to work at the mill until 1917.

# MONOVILLE

On July 4, 1859, Dog Town held Independence Day celebrations. A town resident left the festivities and wandered the hills east of Dog Town. He rested, picked up some dirt, and found it contained gold.

Word of his discovery spread like wildfire, and it was rumored that gold was on the ground for the taking. Most of Dog Town picked up their tents and moved them northeast one mile. Soon, miners from Mono Pass, Carson Valley, and Sonora arrived. The find became the first gold rush east of the Sierra.

Developers laid out streets and parcels. Residents soon replaced tents and dugouts with wood structures, which were "whipsawed." Before long, five sawmills were in operation.

While the location of Monoville was beautiful, it was also isolated and suffered extreme winters. During the first winter, only 150 people remained in Monoville. Little mining occurred as placer nuggets were frozen. Snow started on November 15, 1859, and didn't stop until it was five feet deep.

The spring thaw brought renewed interest in Monoville. The town's population exploded to 1,000. Some report the number was closer to 2,500, consisting of 500 "sober" and 2,000 "intoxicated persons."

Monoville grew to include forty structures, including twenty-two saloons, stores, gambling halls, hotels and boarding houses, and restaurants. One saloon boasted a two-lane bowling alley.

Monoville's downfall was its remote location. The post office closed on April 16, 1862, after only two and a half years of operation. In 1863, the population had decreased to 300. By 1868, town residents abandoned Monoville, and the few remaining buildings suffered from neglect and heavy snow.

# LIME KILN

Buildings with rock, brick, or stone required mortar to cement the stones together. The mortar was made by baking travertine in lime kilns.

Workers quarried travertine from the knoll and loaded it into the top of the kilns. They stacked wood in the bottom of the kiln and set it on fire, baking and drying the travertine. Once finished, they crushed the stone into a fine powder and mixed it with sand and water. The paste was used as mortar, stucco, or plaster for walls and ceilings.

The Bodie & Benton Railway (B&B) had a siding at Lime Kiln. The kiln was twelve miles from Bodie, down a steep grade at the bottom of a complex series of switchbacks. Following the decline of Bodie's mining and milling, the railroad ceased service to the kiln and lumber mill in 1917. The B&B never did extend to Benton.

BODIE AND BENTON R. R.

SURVEYED IN MARCH, 1881, AND COMPLETED IN
DECEMBER, 1881, WITH MATERIALS HAULED FROM
HAWTHORNE, NEVADA, THROUGH BODIE TO THIS
ROAD BED, AT A COST OF ONE MILLION DOLLARS.
THIS NARROW GAUGE RAILWAY CARRIED TIMBER
SUPPLIES 31.74 MILES FROM MONO MILLS TO
BODIE STATION, RISING IN GRADE 2074 FEET TO
AN ELEVATION OF 8500 FEET. OPERATIONS
CONTINUED UNTIL 1918, WHEN DECREASED MINING
ACTIVITY CAUSED THE RAILROAD TO BE DISMANTLED.

DEDICATED SEPTEMBER 13, 1969
BODIE CHAPTER, E CLAMPUS VITUS
MONO COUNTY BOARD OF SUPERVISORS

NEARBY DECHAMBEAU RANCH

# CONWAY RANCHES

I n the 1870s, ranchers James Wilson and Harlan Noyes settled the pastureland below Conway Summit and Mono Lake. Bodie was the largest purchaser of their cattle. John Conway of Bodie purchased the ranch in 1903. They expanded the ranch to include pork, dairy, and hay. In 1907, they started a stage line between Bodie and Lundy. Their house was used as a stage station to provide weary travelers with meals and a place to rest.

Jim Conway died in 1918. His family worked the ranch until the 1980s. A decade later, developers made plans to create housing sites on the ranch. The Eastern Sierra Land Trust worked with governmental agencies to preserve this historic ranch.

# JORDAN

PENSTOCK DAMAGED IN THE AVALANCHE

The Pacific Power Company was founded in 1910 to provide electricity to local mining operations and towns. They built the Jordan Power Plant in 1911 to supply power to Bodie and Aurora. Four cottages around the plant housed eight residents.

The winter of 1910 to 1911 was particularly hard for the Eastern Sierra. Nearby, Lundy had two avalanches. Masonic had one, and Golden Gate to the north had three. Nine miners, including the owner of Masonic, lost their lives in avalanches.

On March 7, 1911, an estimated four million tons of snow slid down Copper Mountain. The avalanche ripped a quarter-mile-wide path, scattering the Jordan Power Plant and houses a mile down the slope.

Jordan's neighboring towns had yet to learn what happened. The snowstorm downed phone lines, and it was not unusual for residents to lose phone services and power in harsh Sierra winters. The following day, the storm broke. Lineman Paul Greenleaf and L.A. Larson left Bodie to find the break in the power line. They followed the line the entire distance and dioscovered the devastation.

Miraculously, there were two survivors. Rescue workers from Lee Vining and Bodie heard the whimpering of a dog coming from the wreckage of cabin number one, belonging to the plant engineer, R.H. Mason. A steamer trunk had prevented the total collapse of a wall and created a shelter and air pocket for Mason's wife, Agnes, and her dog. Rescuers took Agnes to nearby Conway Ranch, then to the hospital in Bodie. She lost her leg to gangrene but survived.

Bodies of seven victims were recovered and moved to Mattley Ranch, where they remained in a cold shed for several weeks until coffins could arrive. A local priest officiated a funeral attended by many of the valley residents. The graves overlook the site of the avalanche. Headstones are reclaimed marble from the power plant switchboard.

VENITA PHOTO BY:
AUSTIN METZ,
NEVADA EXPEDITIONS

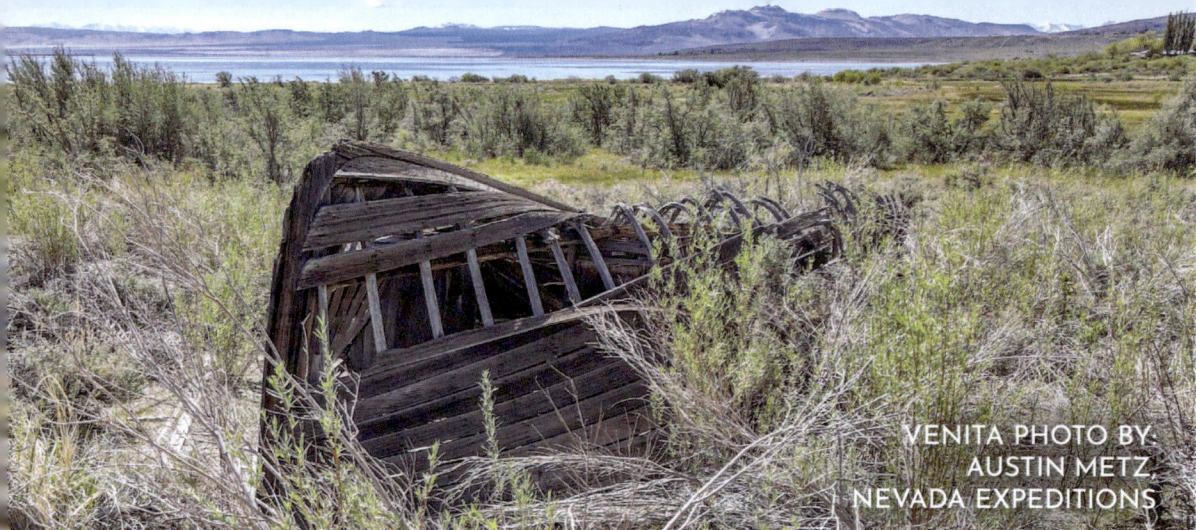

# MONO INN & THE VENITA

Mono Lake became a tourist destination in the early 1900s, and Mono Inn, a hotel and restaurant, opened in 1922. Wally McPherson's parents raised him in the family home on Pahoa Island in Mono Lake. In the early 1930s, he purchased the Mono Inn. The inn operated a thirty-five-foot pleasure craft, the *Venita*, for guest excursions on the lake. In 1950, a winter storm tossed the craft off its dry dock, destroying the *Venita*.

Famed photographer Ansel Adams's family purchased Mono Inn in 1996, converting the property into a gallery and fine dining. The inn closed between 2007 and 2011 but is now known for its beautiful property and farm-to-table dining.

Adeline Carson Stilts, daughter of the famed Kit Carson, was known as "Prairie Flower" by her father. She and her husband moved to Monoville in 1858. As was all too common at the time, she died in childbirth the following year. The family buried her along Mono Lake. The exact site is unknown, but it is on the grounds of what is now the Mono Inn.

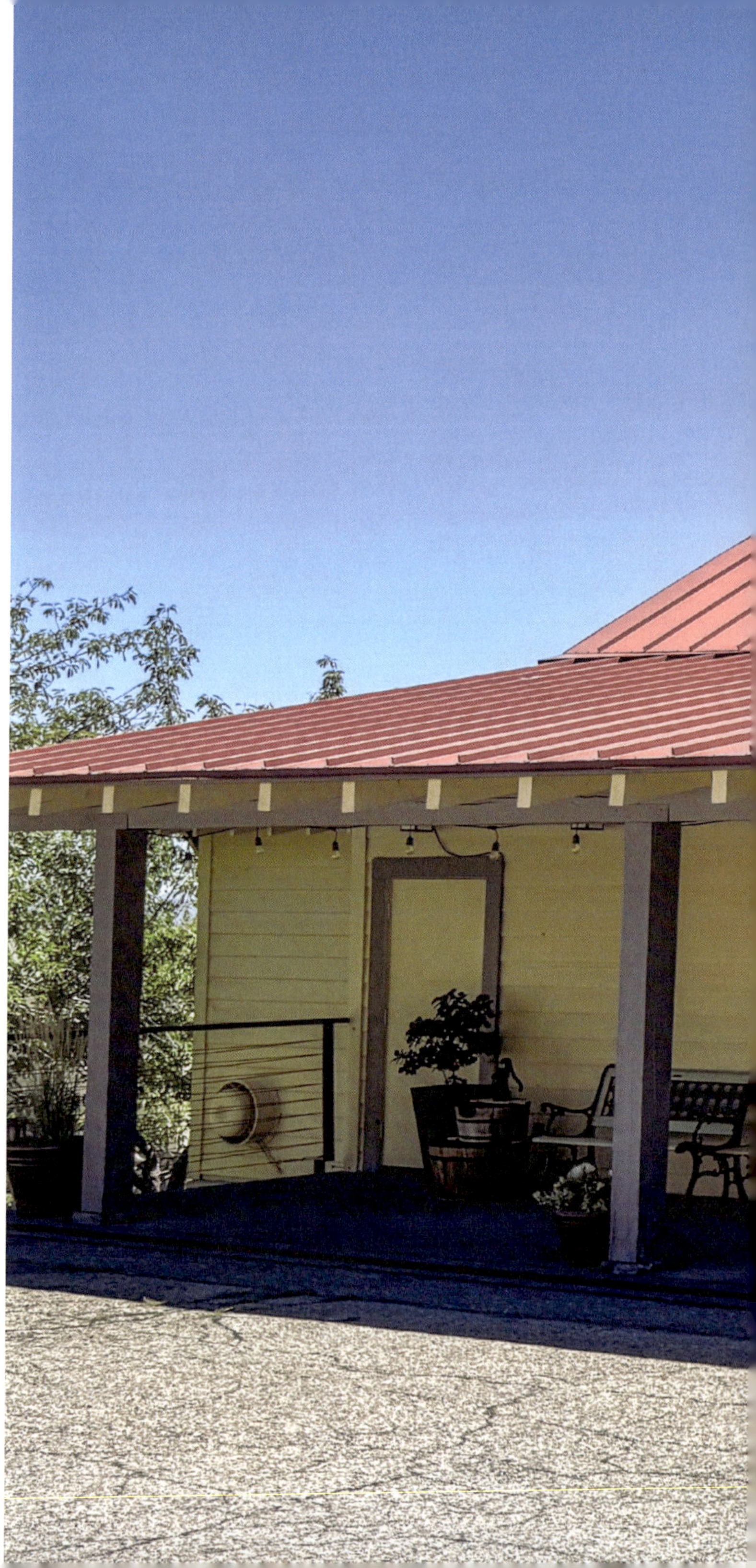

# HAMMOND'S STATION & MONO LAKE

Brothers Jack and Dick Hammond worked at the Sheepherder Mine at Tioga. They purchased the Mono Lake toll gate and store, renaming it Hammond's Station. The post office of Mono opened on March 21, 1882; two years later, it moved to Bodie. In 1889, a post office opened at Mono Lake, with John Mattley as the first postmaster. The office was a single room with cubby holes for the mail.

Mattley was a bachelor, despite his attempts at finding a bride. He was proud of his silver beard, which hung to his knees. Usually pinned up, he left it hanging free at dances in an attempt to woo women. Regardless of the power of his beard, he remained single until he tried a magazine advertisement to find a wife.

Around 1897, owners relocated buildings from Bodie to Mono Lake; they are now the registration and restaurant for Tioga Lodge. In 1908, additional buildings were relocated from Lundy.

Hammond's Station was the center of the Mono Basin. One of the area's only telephones drew residents to the store for updates from the outside world. It was a multifunctional toll station, gambling hall, and, some say, a brothel. They offered high proof "Red Eye," reportedly making those who partook "see double and feel single."

# LOG CABIN MINE

old was discovered in 1890 but not claimed until Jim Simpson obtained the mineral rights in 1910. A company from Washington State purchased Simpson's claim in the 1930s. Forty miners worked at the mine.

At almost 10,000 feet in elevation, Log Cabin Mine experienced brutal winters with up to twenty-five feet of snow. Over winter, supplies were brought in by snowshoe. Sadly, two miners were returning from a St. Patrick's Day celebration in town and froze to death before they could make it back to the mine.

The mine closed in World War II. Operations resumed after the war, but little gold was processed. The facility was maintained until 1968.

# BENTON

Paiute were the first to use the hot springs west of the White Mountains. In 1852, with the mining booms, the springs became a stopping point for travelers. A decade later, with gold and then silver discovered in the surrounding hills, Benton grew and became one of the first towns in Mono County.

Benton became a supply center for the region and, by 1865, had the largest population of any town in Mono County. Services included a Wells Fargo office, butcher, stores, boarding houses, hotels, and saloons; the *Bentonian*, a semi-weekly newspaper operated in the 1880s.

Benton thrived for half a century. Even though most mining ceased by the 1890s, it clung to life. In the 1930s, the Bramlettes purchased the entire town site and preserved the history. Today, Benton is a popular retreat with cabin rentals and campsites.

BLIND SPRING HILL CABIN
RELOCATED TO BENTON

# BLIND SPRING HILL

Prospectors from Montgomery City discovered ore in Blind Spring Hill in 1865 and rapidly filed hundreds of mining claims. Despite the name, there was no water on Blind Spring Hill, so they transported water from Benton Hot Springs.

A mining camp developed, isolated on the mountainside, including a hotel, stores, and saloons. Due to a lack of water, most miners lived closer to the hot springs.

Many miners at Blind Spring Hill were Chinese or Native Americans. Blind Spring Hill was progressive for the times. In 1876, white miners refused to eat at the same table as the Chinese workers. The foreman told the miners that if they didn't like it, they could collect their pay and leave.

# MONTGOMERY CITY

The short-lived mining camp of Montgomery City started in the early 1860s when prospectors found rich silver floats along the western slope of the White Mountains.

A town grew alongside a stream, and several hundred people called Montgomery City home. The town had lumber and stone buildings, including a store, saloon, blacksmith shop, recorder's office, and homes. Pat Reddy was a mining recorder at Montgomery City. He later became a criminal lawyer in Bodie.

Montgomery City was home to the first newspaper in Mono County, *The Montgomery Pioneer*. The paper printed the first issue on November 26, 1864.

Sitting at the mouth of the steep White Mountains, Montgomery City was subject to flash floods. In one case, millions of gallons of water and rocks slid down the mountains. Miraculously, the loss of life was "small."

The winter of 1864 was long and arduous, and "grub" ran short. One Thompson owned a pack train business. A sober-looking little donkey was his pride and joy. Miners developed a plan: steal the donkey on Christmas Eve and BBQ it for a Christmas celebration. Word of the "Murderous Intentions" reached Thompson, and he hid the young jack before the would-be kidnappers arrived. Men cried and swore vengeance against the traitor who spoiled their Christmas festivities.

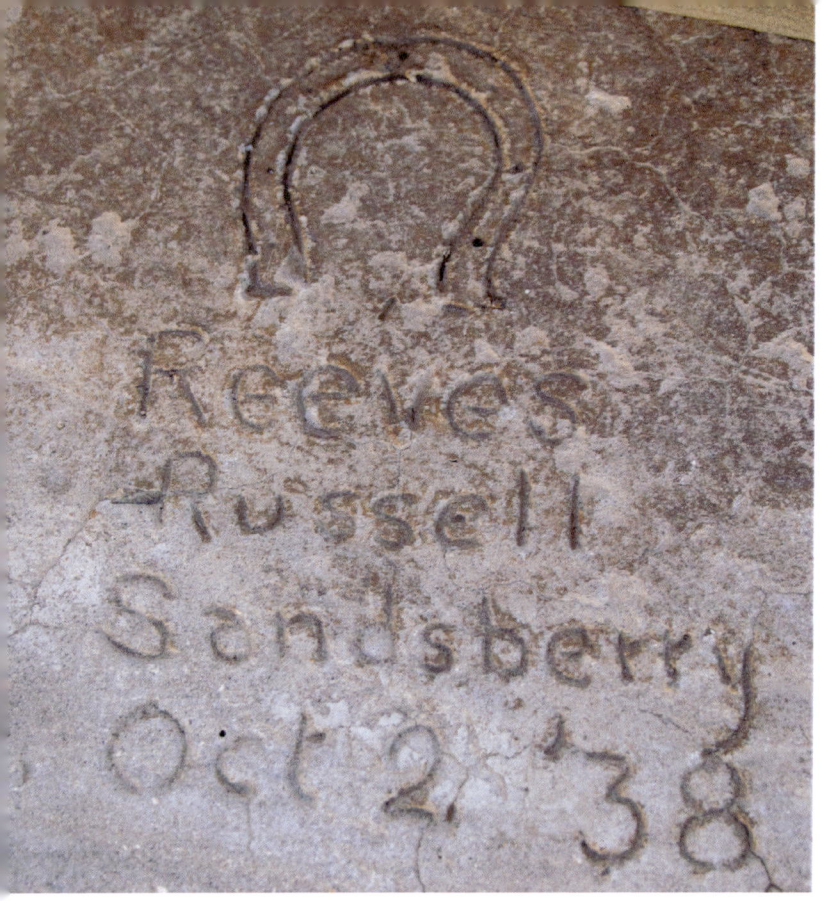

AERIAL TRAMWAY

# SACRAMENTO MINE

The Sacramento Mine was initially worked by prospectors from Mexico in the 1870s. They carried ore on their backs to an arrastra, a primitive drag-stone mill. They worked the claim until 1878.

A variety of companies worked in the mine for over a century. The Rowland Brothers leased the mine following foreclosure. They employed ten men with plans to continue operations. In 1912, the White Mountain Mining Company assumed control of the Sacramento Mill.

An aerial tram was constructed in 1938. Reeves Russell Sandsberry left his mark in the concrete on October 2. In 1965, a company again made plans to work the Sacramento Mine with a five-stamp mill. Within a year, sixteen men were working for the mine, with an expected addition of men.

# TOM PUMICE MILL

In 1927, the California Quarries Company mined and milled pumice for soap and building materials. A tram carried the bagged pumice to a rail station called Tom on the Carson & Colorado Railroad (C&C).

In the early 1930s, the C&C applied to abandon the line to Tom as the mill only produced enough to need a weekly trip. The request was denied, and the rail continued running until 1938. The rail lines survived until 1942, when they were removed for the war effort. Insulating Aggregates, Inc. purchased the mill in 1947 and installed a seventy-ton mill.

KNIGHT WHEEL

# MAMMOTH

Four prospectors found a claim on Mineral Hill in 1877, and the Mammoth Mining Company was established the following year. By the end of the year, 1,500 people had moved to the new mining camp.

In 1878, a twenty-stamp mill operated at nearby Mill City. A mule team relocated a Knight Wheel from Mojave to power the mill. The Knight Wheel is a Pelton-style wheel, but the turbine generated more power with less water. Within a decade, mining ceased, and the camp was abandoned except for a handful of people. In 1902, the Knight Wheel moved again to produce electricity for the Wildasinn Hotel, and later Charlie Summer's Mammoth Camp as Mammoth became a tourist destination.

Life around Mammoth was difficult. In 1882, Julia Townsend, wife of Bryant and mother of three, died during the heavy winter. As the ground was frozen and covered in snow, the family couldn't bury her until the thaw. She once dreamed of having a home with a white picket fence. Unable to fulfill her dream during her lifetime, her husband built a white picket fence around her grave.

# MAMMOTH CONSOLIDATED MINE CAMP

A.G. Mahan, his son Arch, and several partners purchased many of the 1877 Red Mountain mining claims, forming the Mammoth Consolidated Mine Company. The mine operated between 1927 and 1933, producing only $100,000 of gold ($2.5 million in 2025). It was the last significant mining effort in the area.

Up to fourteen men lived and worked at Mammoth Consolidated Camp. They earned around $4 a day ($75 in 2025). They lived in rustic bunkhouses with no electricity. Isolated from civilization, the camp included mine offices, an assay office, a school, cabins, and the mill.

In 1934, Mahan transitioned to the tourism industry and purchased Reds Meadow Pack Station. Today, the US Forest Service preserves the camp in a state of "arrested decay." The remaining structures include Mahan's cabin, bunkhouses, and equipment from the diesel-powered mill.

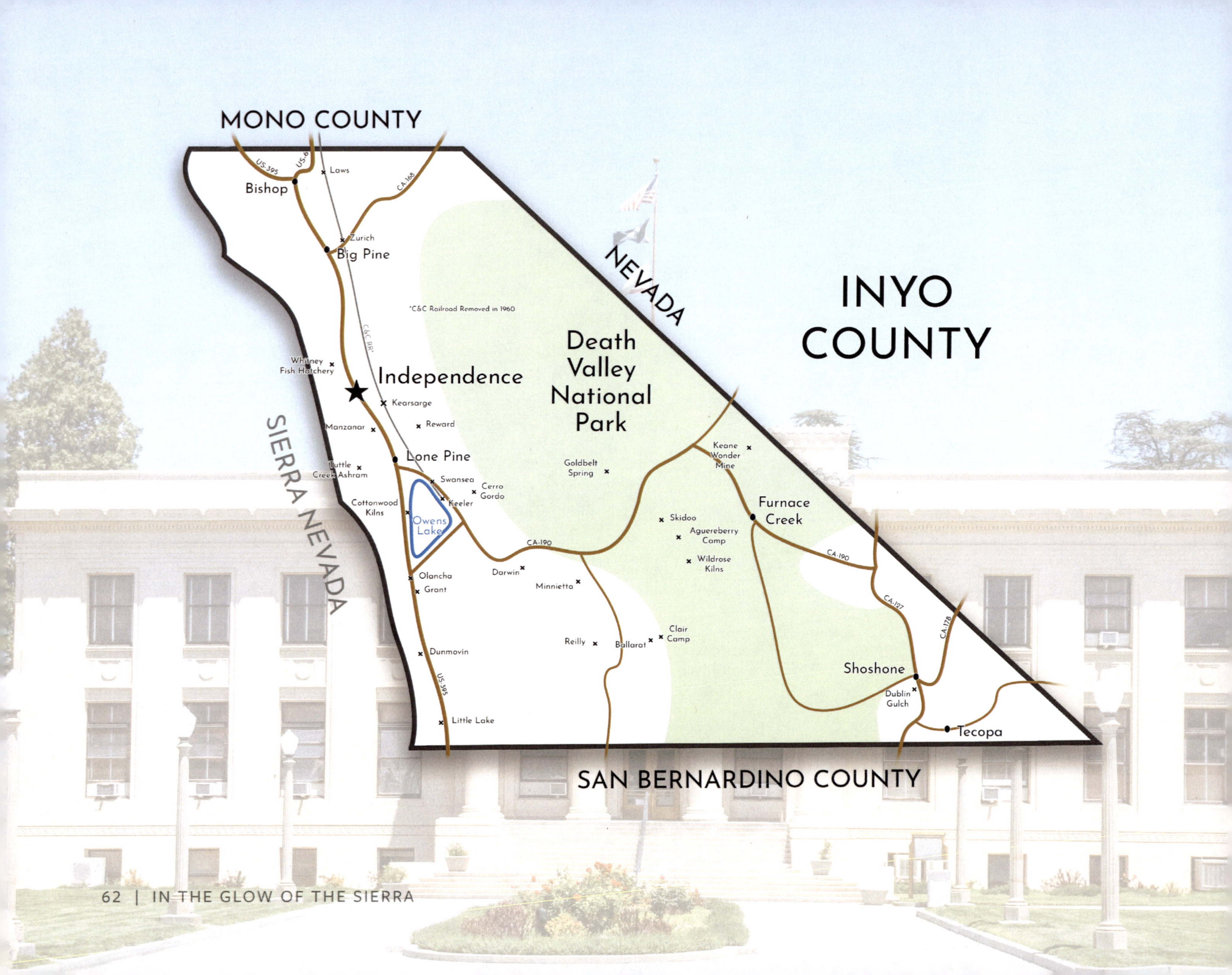

MONO COUNTY

INYO COUNTY

NEVADA

SIERRA NEVADA

*C&C Railroad Removed in 1960

US-395  US-6  CA-168

Bishop
Laws

Zurich
Big Pine

C&C RR*

Whitney
Fish Hatchery

Independence

Death
Valley
National
Park

Kearsarge

Reward

Manzanar

Lone Pine

Goldbelt
Spring

Keane
Wonder
Mine

Tuttle
Creek Ashram

Swansea

Cerro
Gordo

Cottonwood
Kilns

Keeler

Owens
Lake

CA-190

Skidoo

Furnace
Creek

Aguereberry
Camp

CA-190

Darwin

Wildrose
Kilns

Olancha

Minnietta

CA-127

Grant

CA-178

Reilly
Ballarat

Clair
Camp

Dunmovin

Shoshone

US-395

Dublin
Gulch

Little Lake

Tecopa

SAN BERNARDINO COUNTY

# Chapter Two: INYO

## The California Legislature created Inyo County in 1866 from the unorganized Coso County. In 1870, Inyo acquired land from Mono County, and in 1872 from San Bernardino.

Inyo County is the traditional land for four tribes: the Mono tribe, the Coso people, the Timbisha, and the Kawaiisu Native Americans. The name Inyo has two stories. First, it comes from the Mono language and means "dwelling place of great spirit." The second is from Inyo, head of the Timbisha band. When early settlers asked the name of the mountains to the east, the tribe told them Inyo. The pioneers believed Inyo was the name of the range, not realizing Inyo was the head of the tribe and that the lands belonged to Inyo's tribe.

Inyo is the second-largest county in California, yet it has the second-lowest population density. Death Valley National Monument was created in 1933, and half of Inyo County is in the park.

Independence is the county seat of Inyo. In 1861, Charles Putnam opened a trading post known as Putman's and later Little Pine. Two miles from town, the US Army established Camp Independence to protect settlers from disputes with Native Americans. A post office opened in 1866, and was renamed after Camp Independence.

Mining built Inyo County. In 1865, Cerro Gordo sprang to life following the discovery of silver ore. The new settlement would become California's version of Virginia City, Nevada. Multiple settlements, mills, and transportation systems were born to support the legendary town. Cerro Gordo's need for supplies and shipping was so vast that the City of Los Angeles grew to meet the demand. The *Los Angeles News* wrote, "What Los Angeles is, is mainly due to it (Cerro Gordo). It is the silver cord that binds our present existence."

On March 26, 1872, the Lone Pine earthquake shook Owens Valley. At an estimated 7.4 to 7.9 magnitude, it was one of the largest earthquakes to hit California. The earthquake forever changed Inyo County. Twenty-six people lost their lives. Major buildings in most of Inyo's towns fell. Camp Independence was in ruins. The shoreline of Owens Lake rose, making the piers at Swansea useless.

Inyo County suffered $250,000 in damages (over $6.5 million in 2025). Most buildings were adobe, which did not withstand the quake. Settlers rallied to help their communities and those in need. Cerro Gordo escaped significant damage but raised $800 ($20,000 in 2025) to help repair or restore Inyo's towns. Structures were rebuilt using wood construction.

On July 4, 1872, Inyo County celebrated Independence Day festivities. A fortunate few rode the steamship *Bessie Brady* across Owens Lake to enjoy a picnic.

Life in Inyo moved on and grew from supporting mining to agriculture and tourism.

# LAWS

In 1861, four ranchers arrived in Owens Valley and built a sod and stone house along the Owens River. Two years later, the mining camp of Owensville grew to support mines in the White Mountains. Mining declined after a decade, and residents abandoned Owensville.

The Carson & Colorado Railroad (C&C) created Bishop Station at the former Owensville townsite as an agricultural, mining, and shipping transportation center. A post office opened in 1887, and the town included stores, a boarding house, restaurants, a blacksmith, a dance hall, and a school.

In 1900, the Southern Pacific Railroad purchased the C&C, renaming the town after a railroad official, R.J. Laws. The town of Laws declined with the Great Depression. In 1938, Southern Pacific removed the line north of town, but the station at Laws remained active as the northern terminus in Owens Valley. The rail line south of Laws ceased operation in 1960, and the post office closed three years later. Laws milled clay and talc from local mines throughout the decade.

Hollywood helped preserve Laws. Inyo County wanted to open a railroad museum, and movie producers wanted to use Laws to film the movie, *Nevada Smith*. The partners restored buildings, relocated others around the area, and added more to create a scenic town. In 1966, *Nevada Smith* made its debut, and the Laws Railroad Museum opened.

# ZURICH STATION

Known initially as Alford, Zurich was a Carson & Colorado Railroad freight and passenger station beginning in 1884. The station was the first south of Laws and became a transportation hub for locations east of Big Pine, with teamsters hauling passengers and freight the three miles from town. Zurich included a siding station, railroad buildings, and an agent's house.

The rail agent's wife, Emilie Kikolaus, was from Zurich, Switzerland. She fell in love with the snow-covered Sierra and wanted to rename the station in honor of her hometown. Her husband was an intelligent man, and to satisfy his wife, he promptly renamed Alford to Zurich Station in 1923.

Zurich Station closed in 1960 when the railroad discontinued service.

# WHITNEY FISH HATCHERY

The California State Fish and Game Commission built the Whitney Fish Hatchery in 1917 to raise trout for the Eastern Sierra. California golden trout eggs were collected at Rae Lakes and later at Cottonwood Lakes.

The buildings are built from local granite in the Tudor Revival style. The hatchery included 120 troughs and could raise three million fingerlings.

Fire, followed by thunderstorms, severely damaged the grounds in 2008. The focus changed from a hatchery to education and preservation. Owned by the California Department of Fish and Wildlife, Friends of Mt. Whitney Fish Hatchery assumed control of the fish hatchery and operations.

# KEARSARGE STATION

In 1864, five woodcutters discovered silver and other ore. They began working their mining claims, and they shipped four tons to a stamp mill in Nevada. Investors formed the Kearsarge Mining Company, and Kearsarge City soon had over 1,000 residents. The town hoped to become the county seat of Inyo in the next election but lost to Independence. In 1866, an avalanche destroyed much of Kearsarge, killing the foreman's wife and injuring others.

In the valley below, Kearsarge stagecoach station opened in 1866. In 1883, the Carson & Colorado Railroad expanded its facilities and opened Kearsarge Station. Workers lived in a bunkhouse, and the boss lived in a house. The station closed in 1932 and was dismantled in 1952.

Karsarge's name was born from the Civil War. Nearby southern sympathizers named Alabama Hills to honor the accomplishments of the Confederate warship, the CSS *Alabama*.

The CSS *Alabama* sank off the coast of France in 1864. Kearsage was named after the Union man-o-war USS *Kearsage*, which sank the *Alabama*. The town believed the name "evened the score."

# REWARD

Prospectors discovered the Eclipse Mine in 1878. It was worked sporadically from 1880 to 1936, and a small mining camp developed.

The Reward Consolidated Mining Company operated the mine and changed the name to Reward. The town became a supply center for local mines, and a post office was open from 1900 to 1906. Miners shipped ore to the Tropico Mill at Rosamond and later processed on site with a small mill. The Reward Mine was worked through 1960.

# MANZANAR

In early 1942, only months after the Japanese attack on Pearl Harbor, Franklin D. Roosevelt signed an executive order to remove "any or all persons" of Japanese descent from prescribed military areas on the West Coast. The order created ten war relocation centers for the banned individuals.

Over 120,000 Americans of Japanese descent, including men, women, and children, were forced to abandon their personal property and move to the military-style camps. Two-thirds were native-born Americans, and many of the others were denied American citizenship under federal law.

Manzanar was the first camp to open; the first detainees arrived in March 1942. By July, over 10,000 Japanese Americans were incarcerated, most from Los Angeles. The camp covered over 500 acres. It was fenced by barbed wire and surrounded by eight towers filled with guards armed with machine guns. In December, a riot occurred, ending in the death of two inmates.

Despite their forced incarceration based solely on their heritage, detainees created as normal of a town as they could, including stores, a newspaper, beauty salons, beautiful water gardens, sports, and recreational activities.

Over 145 individuals died while incarcerated at Manzanar, including seventeen-year-old James Ito and twenty-one-year-old Jim Kanagawa, who were shot and killed in the "Manzanar Riot."

Manzanar closed on November 21, 1945. Despite losing almost everything and having been forcibly brought to Owens Valley, detainees were given $25 ($500 in 2025) and a bus or train ticket and told to leave.

# MANZANAR CHILDREN'S VILLAGE

Manzanar was the only war relocation center with an orphanage. Children, ages newborn to eighteen, were taken from foster homes, orphanages, and unwed mothers and placed in Manzanar Children's Village. In June 1942, sixty-one children from orphanages and foster care arrived by bus at Manzanar. Eventually, 101 children would live in the children's village.

Manzanar Children's Village was a camp within a camp; it was part of Manzanar but separate. Built on an old pear field across from the hospital, the village consisted of three one-story buildings. One building housed caregivers in apartments and included a recreation center, a kitchen, and a dining room. The second building housed infants, young children, and girls; the third building was for boys and a storeroom. Unlike the family barracks, the children's village had running water and bathrooms. The village had lawns, trees, and flowers. The staff built a playground and gazebos. Some residents of Owens Valley baked cookies and brought the children clothing and toys.

For many residents of the Manzanar Children's Village, the most challenging time came with the camp's closing. The children and staff were the only family they knew. Many had spent their entire life in institutionalized care and never lived in traditional family units. The orphanages did not reopen following World War II, resulting in the children being separated and placed with extended family, in foster or group homes, or placed for adoption. In September of 1945, the last children left the children's village.

In his final report of the internment camp in 1946, Ralph P. Merritt, Manzanar's top official, wrote *"What a travesty [of] justice!"*

ADOBE WALL OF THE MEYSAN'S STORE

# LONE PINE

The Paiutes first inhabited Owens Valley and established trading routes with other tribes. The first non-native settler built a cabin between 1860 and 1862. Over the next few years, a settlement developed named Lone Pine. It was named for a single Jeffrey pine tree growing at the mouth of the canyon. Lone Pine became a trading and supply center for gold and silver mines in the Alabama Hills. A post office opened in 1870, and the town included eighty buildings, mainly constructed from adobe.

On March 26, 1872, the Lone Pine earthquake shook Owens Valley. The epicenter was at Lone Pine. At an estimated 7.4 to 7.9 magnitude, it was one of the largest earthquakes to hit California. Sixty buildings fell; the twenty that survived were wood constructions. Twenty-six people lost their lives.

Only one adobe wall survived the quake: the general merchandise store owned by Charles and Madeline Meysan. The French couple and their children moved to Lone Pine in 1869 and opened the first store on the west side of Main Street. Their daughter Alice developed eye problems, and in March of 1872, Charles and Alice left to visit a doctor. Alice was so homesick that Charles returned to Lone Pine. Three weeks later, Alice was killed in the earthquake when the adobe wall collapsed on her. Her parents buried her in a mass grave along with fifteen others.

Lone Pine was home to transient miners, workers on the Los Angeles Aqueduct, and film crews for more than 500 movies and television episodes filmed in the Alabama Hills. Today, it is the gateway for those climbing Mt. Whitney, the tallest mountain in the continental United States.

# TUTTLE CREEK ASHRAM

Frank Merrell-Wolff and his wife, Sherifa "Sara" Merrell, were told by an "Old Indian" that the most spiritual place is the highest point. Since Mt. Whitney was the highest point in the US before Alaska gained statehood, the Merrells traveled to Owens Valley. Falling in love with the natural beauty, they camped for two months. The couple wrote books on transcendental philosophy, mysticism, and "esoteric Hinduism." They were inspired to create an ashram, a non-denominational place of worship and religious study.

The Merrells wanted to build the ashram at the base of Mt. Whitney, but obtained permission to build at Tuttle Creek instead. Construction began in 1928 with blasting to form a foundation. The couple and their followers worked on the ashram for twenty years but never finished the structure.

Volunteers and the Merrells constructed an ashram out of local stone. Burros carried concrete mix up the steep road daily. The church is in the shape of a balanced cross, representing equilibrium and aligned in the four compass directions.

Work ceased in 1950 as Sara could no longer make the trip up the Sierra. In 1964, the Tuttle Creek Ashram became part of the John Muir Wilderness. New regulations disallowed buildings in a wilderness area. The US Forest Service planned to destroy the structures, but they saved the ashram due to its historical significance.

THE MILL AT SWANSEA

# SWANSEA

In 1869, Colonel Sherman Stevens built the Owens Lake Silver-Lead furnace mill to process ore from nearby Cerro Gordo. James Brady bought the mill in 1870. He named the town after Swansea, South Wales, the world leader in gold and silver smelting.

Between 1869 and 1874, Swansea became the center for smelting and transporting ore. A pier allowed ore to be transported on the steamship *Bessie Brady* across Owens Lake to Cartago, decreasing travel time from three days to three hours.

The Lone Pine earthquake in 1872 damaged the smelters at Swansea. The land shifted, raising the shoreline of Owens Lake and preventing steamships from accessing Swansea's pier. Most operations shifted a mile south to Keeler. In 1874, thunderstorms caused flash flooding, leaving Swansea under several feet of rock and sand, ending the town.

# KEELER

Following the destruction of Swansea's pier in 1872, shipping and most businesses moved one mile south to Hawley, where they built a new wharf. In 1879, the Owens Lake Mining and Milling Company constructed a new mill to process ore from Cerro Gordo. Company agent Captain Keeler planned a town named after himself.

Keeler had a 300-foot pier for the steamship *Bessie Brady*. She could cross Owens Lake in three hours, transporting 700 ingots. In 1882, a fire destroyed the *Bessie Brady*. Fortunately, in 1883, the Carson & Colorado Railroad (C&C) arrived in Keeler, allowing transportation between the mines and the smelter.

The town thrived with the silver boom in Cerro Gordo. Keeler declined with the passage of the Coinage Act of 1873, which shifted the United States' monetary system to a gold standard.

A revival in zinc mining occurred in early 1907. An aerial tram transported ore from the mines to Keeler's mills. The final product was shipped on the C&C.

The Natural Soda Products Company began harvesting baking soda from Owens Lake to use in laundry detergent. In the early 1900s, over 7,000 people lived in Keeler, which included hotels, boarding houses, and stores. Keeler built "The Plunge," Owens Valley's first swimming pool. Mining ended in the 1950s, and in 1960, the C&C ended service to Keeler. With the aqueduct draining Owens Lake dry, alkali dust storms drove away most residents.

CARSON & COLORADO DEPOT

# CERRO GORDO

Pablo Flores, a miner from Mexico, discovered galena, a silver-lead ore, above the Owens Valley in 1865. The mines were named Cerro Gordo, which is Spanish for "Fat Hill." Word spread, and by 1866, a settlement had been formed. Victor Beaudry of Independence saw potential and opened the first store. Beaudry assumed multiple mining claims from miners to settle their debts and constructed two smelters to process ore. As miners accumulated more unpaid debt, Beaudry continued to acquire more claims until he owned the majority of the mines in Cerro Gordo.

Cerro Gordo became California's largest silver and lead producer within three years. Mule teams transported silver between Cerro Gordo and Los Angeles. While smelters processed ore on site, mines shipped most ore via wagons and steamships across Owens Lake from Swansea and Keeler.

Starting in 1875, Cerro Gordo suffered multiple setbacks. Ore ledges played out, the water supply dried up, the mines faced legal issues, and in 1877, a fire raged through several mines. The final straw for Cerro Gordo was falling silver prices. A decade after Cerro Gordo sprang to life, many residents moved in search of the next big strike.

Cerro Gordo was a "wide-open town" known for frequent gunfights and little law enforcement. Dr. Hugh K. McCelland attended a dance hall one evening for pleasure instead of his usual visits to treat the wounds from fights. Another attendee asked the doctor the name of a prostitute, and he replied with her nickname, "The Horned Toad." Hearing the unflattering name, The Horned Toad drew her dagger to attack. "The Fenian," an independent prostitute known for her charitable acts, grabbed The Horned Toad's wrist, preventing the attack. A friend of the Toad drew his knife to avenge the use of the name. George Snow, a prominent miner, pulled out his revolver, shooting the attacker before he could injure the doctor. A gunfight erupted, and shooting continued until the dance hall extinguished the lights.

# DARWIN

Darwin French was a "man of adventure," a physician, soldier, and silver prospector. In 1860, French led a group into Death Valley to search for the mythical Gunsight Lode. A town grew west of Death Valley in 1874, and the residents named it in honor of French. The Darwin post office opened in 1875, and the town became a supply center for mines in the Coso and Argus ranges. Services included hotels, pharmacies, restaurants, a newspaper, and enough saloons to quench the thirst of miners. Two smelters and twenty mines operated around Darwin.

Darwin soon grew to be the largest population center in Inyo County. Due to its isolated location from the county seat in Independence, gunfights and stage robberies occurred routinely in Darwin. At its height in 1877, Darwin sheltered over 3,500 residents. Tragically, in 1878, smallpox ravaged the town.

Soon after the epidemic, mining declined, and many moved to join the mining boom in Bodie. In 1879, a fire destroyed the Darwin Hotel and much of the business district.

A mining revival in the early 1900s breathed new life into Darwin. Mines reworked previous tailings and discovered new deposits. They shipped ore to Salt Lake City and Keeler. Darwin was rebuilt, including a new hotel. Tragically, fire again swept through Darwin in 1917 and 1918, destroying the hotel, saloons, and homes.

In 1926, the Eichbaum Toll Road connected Death Valley to the west, and Darwin provided services for travelers. Tourist dollars and mining seemed to assure Darwin's future.

In 1933, Death Valley became a national monument. Four years later, a new cutoff provided access to Death Valley, bypassing Darwin. A handful of residents still call Darwin home.

# MINNIETTA

Following the success of Lookout City, prospectors expanded their search and discovered mines farther down the peak. In 1876, mining began at Minnietta Star Belle Mine, followed soon by the Keystone and Mountain View Mines. The ore at Minnietta was rich, assaying at 200 ounces of silver per ton, with some gold.

Famed teamster, Remi Nadeau constructed a road from Panamint Valley to the Minnietta Mine. His mule-driven wagons brought ore to the mills at Surprise Valley and returned with charcoal from the Wildrose Kilns. The ore eventually ran out, and the mine was foreclosed in 1877.

In 1883, Jack Gunn purchased the mines. Gunn worked the mine continuously until 1905, then periodically for another decade. In thirty-two years, Gunn produced $500,000 in silver and gold ($18 million in 2025).

Minnietta was leased in the 1930s, and new equipment was installed to reprocess tailings. The mine remained in the Gunn family until 1946 and was worked into the 1990s. In 114 years, Minnietta produced over $1 million (approximately $34 million in 2025) in silver, gold, copper, zinc, and lead.

Sadly, much of Minnietta was destroyed. Around 1990, vandals blew up the bunkhouse and mess hall using stolen dynamite. The superintendent's house survived and became part of BLMs' "Adopt a Cabin" program. Volunteers lovingly restored and maintained the cabin. It is available for people to stay at on a first come, first serve basis.

# SKIDOO

Miners formed a settlement in 1906 near the Skidoo Mine in the Panamint Range. The post office opened under the name Hoveck in 1907; it was named after the Vice President of the Skidoo Townsite and Mining Company. The settlement's name changed to Skidoo in 1907, a slang term in the early 1900s meaning to leave quickly or skedaddle.

Seven hundred called Skidoo home. Many lived in tents, the fortunate few in wood buildings. The town included hotels, restaurants, stores, and a newspaper.

The Skidoo Mill was the only desert mill powered by water, piped twenty-one miles from Telescope Peak. The mill had a fifteen-stamps and used cyanide. Between 1907 and 1917, the Skidoo mine produced $1.5 million ($37 million in 2025). Following the mill's closure, Skidoo quickly folded, living up to its name.

Skidoo is the only site in Death Valley where a hanging occurred. Saloon owner, Hootch Simpson fell on hard times and attempted to rob a bank located in a store. Meeting with failure, Hootch returned and killed the store's owner. In the middle of the night, a Skidoo lynch mob located Hootch. They hanged him twice, once in the lynching and the second time for newspaper photographers.

# AGUEREBERRY CAMP & HARRISBURG

Famed Death Valley prospector Frank "Shorty" Harris and his friend, Pete Aguereberry, staked gold claims in the Panamint Range in 1905. Shorty had a reputation for being able to "smell gold." He discovered many famous mines, including the Bullfrog Mine in Nevada. Shorty never worked the mines himself; he preferred saloons to hard work.

As Aguereberry remained behind at their Eureka Mine at "Harrisberry," Shorty and his mule traveled to record their claim. Thanks to Shorty's beloved saloons, word spread rapidly, and soon, 300 called the new settlement home. As reports spread, the town became known as Harrisburg. It never grew beyond a tent city. Discoveries at nearby Skidoo drew miners away.

Aguereberry continued to work the Eureka. In 1907, he built a trio of cabins, taking the cabin on the right for himself. He continued to work his mining claims alone until he died in 1945.

# WILDROSE KILNS

In 1877, a company man only known to history as Morris, headed the Modock Consolidated Mining Company, which built ten beehive charcoal kilns in Wildrose Canyon to fuel the Modoc mills.

Native American, Chinese, and Mexican workers provided labor for the construction and operation of the kilns. Each kiln was twenty-five feet tall and built of limestone with lime, sand, and gravel for mortar.

Forty men worked the kilns. They lived in tents or log cabins by the kilns or at Wildrose Spring. Workers transported charcoal to the Modoc and Minnietta Belle. Jackass pack trains traversed the twenty-five-mile trail.

The Wildrose Kilns operated for only two years. Due to their short lifespan, remote location, and inclusion in Death Valley National Park, the kilns are the best preserved on the West Coast.

# GOLDBELT SPRING

The Western Shoshone Tuhu Band was the first to use Goldbelt Spring, the only reliable spring in the area.

In 1904, legendary Shorty Harris discovered gold near the spring, and others soon staked their claims. The ore was high-grade, spurring hopes for a bonanza and plans for a town. Exploration expanded in 1905 with little result. Miners worked small claims until 1910.

In July 1931, Burro Bill, his wife Edna Price, and her sister Gladys began a hike from Owens Valley to Darwin via Goldbelt Spring. On their journey, they arrived at a spring where John Hunter was camped with his family. Concerned, Hunter asked why they were walking instead of riding. Hunter said, "White men walk sometimes. Indian walk. Squaw walk too. White women never walk."

Concerned about the trio of hikers, Hunter checked on them at Goldbelt Spring and warned them, "Maybe you die." Each night of their journey, Hunter arrived on horseback, checking on the hikers. Intrigued by Gladys's boots, he offered in exchange a beautiful Native American woven basket. Gladys declined the offer each night as they had not finished the hike. The trio finally arrived at their destination, Darwin. Hunter again appeared, still wanting the boots. Gladys changed into tennis shoes, giving Hunter the well-worn boots.

After World War I increased the price of tungsten, Shorty Harris again explored the area around Goldbelt Spring. He mined several hundred pounds of tungsten. The district was periodically worked through the 1960s.

DEATH VALLEY

# KEANE WONDER MINE

In 1904, Jack Keane and Domingo Etcharren, "the one-eyed Basque butcher of Ballarat," searched for silver deposits on the east side of Death Valley. Etcharren abandoned the search, but Keane continued to scout the area. Instead of silver ore, he located a ledge of gold ore. John F. Campbell and his backers purchased the Keane Wonder Mine in 1906.

The Great Earthquake of 1906 in San Francisco had far-reaching effects. The estimated 7.9 to 8.3 magnitude earthquake and resulting fires destroyed 80% of San Francisco, and over 3000 people lost their lives. Campbell lost most of his assets, and improvements to the Keane Wonder Mine ceased. Sildman Consolidated Mines Company purchased the mine in August 1906 and invested about $85,000 in the mill ($300,000 in 2025). They added a twenty-stamp mill, concentration tables, and cyanide processing.

To transport ore from the mine to the mill, they installed a 2,000-foot aerial tramway. The tram consisted of two terminals, twelve towers, and automatically loaded ore buckets capable of carrying 600 pounds each. During peak production, the tramway would transport seventy tons of ore per day.

Structures at the mill included a bunkhouse, cookhouse, mess hall, and offices. High temperatures made operating the mill difficult. Morning temperatures could reach over 110 degrees and could exceed 124 degrees by noon. Miners were often forced to work at night.

The mine was sold several times between 1935 and 1969, but it never saw any significant operation. The final sale was to the National Park Service in the early 1970s for $1.1M ($9 million in 2025).

# COTTONWOOD KILNS

The mines and mills in Cerro Gordo required massive fuel and lumber to operate. Charcoal is more efficient to burn than lumber since it burns slower and hotter, and it weighs less to make transport easier. Following deforestation around town, mines turned their eyes across Owens Valley to Cottonwood Creek.

Charcoal kilns heat wood in a controlled manner for over a week, creating charcoal. Many kilns are constructed from brick and stone, while the Cottonwood Kilns are constructed of clay brick covered in plaster. Vents at the bottom allow for control of the fire.

In 1873, Colonel Sherman Stevens opened a sawmill near the kilns. Lumber was used in the mines and buildings. Charcoal from the Cottonwood Kilns and lumber from the mill were transported to Stevens Wharf, where the steamships, *Bessie Brady* and *Millie Stevens*, crossed Owens Lake to Keeler. These commodities continued their journey on wagons pulled by horses and mules.

# OLANCHA AND GRANT

Working for the Silver Mountain Mining Company, Minnard Farley built an eight-stamp mill in 1863 at the southern end of Owens Lake. The mill and furnace were the first in the Owens Valley. In 1867, during fighting between white settlers and Native Americans, arson destroyed the mill.

Olancha became a stage station between Cerro Gordo and Los Angeles. In 1910, the Southern Pacific Railroad arrived at Olancha with their standard gauge Jawbone Branch. The Roosevelt Midland Trail for automobiles stretched from Washington, DC, to Los Angeles through Olancha. Businesses and services grew to serve rail and automobile travelers and the local farms.

Southern Pacific abandoned the Jawbone line in 1980. As vehicles became more efficient, travelers needed fewer stops. Businesses moved on, and Olancha declined, but a few souls remained.

In 1945, two miles south of Olancha, John Grant opened a gas station, store, airstrip, and motel. The area of Grant changed hands multiple times. The Twilight Zone used the Airflite Café in season two, episode twenty-three, "A Hundred Yards Over the Rim."

A few miles east of Olancha is Dirty Socks Hot Springs. The hot water artesian well was discovered in 1917 while digging a fresh-water well. A decade later, developers built a concrete pool, and buildings for a resort. In 1927, the resort was demolished.

Legend has it that miners from Cerro Gordo bathed in the springs once a year, whether they needed it or not. They washed their dirty socks in the spring, some believed, giving the water its fragrant scent.

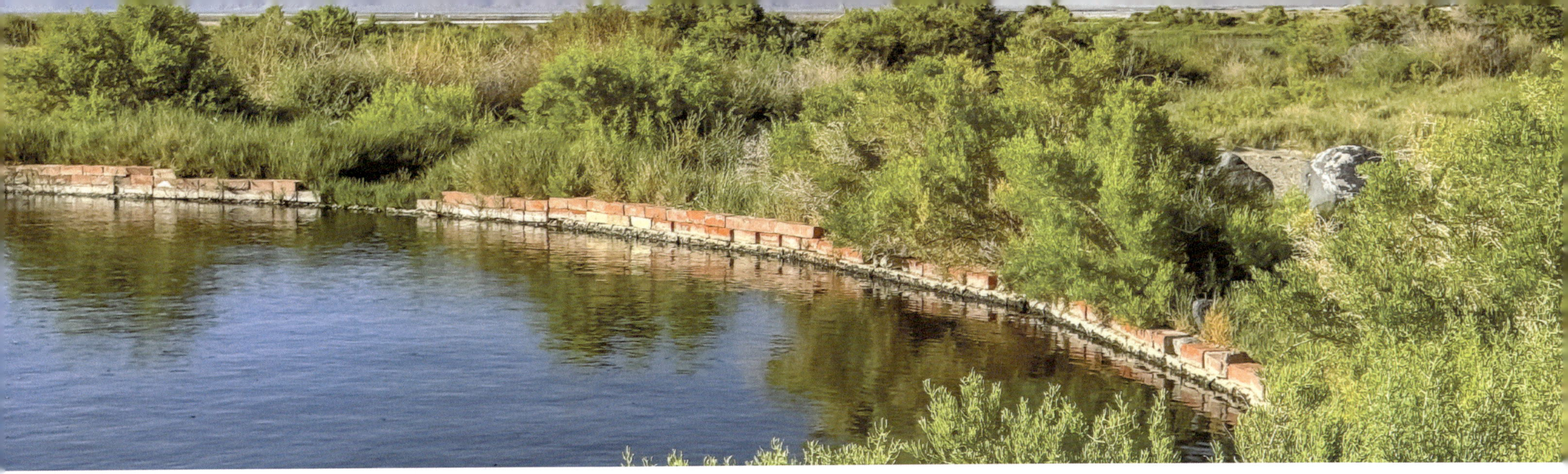

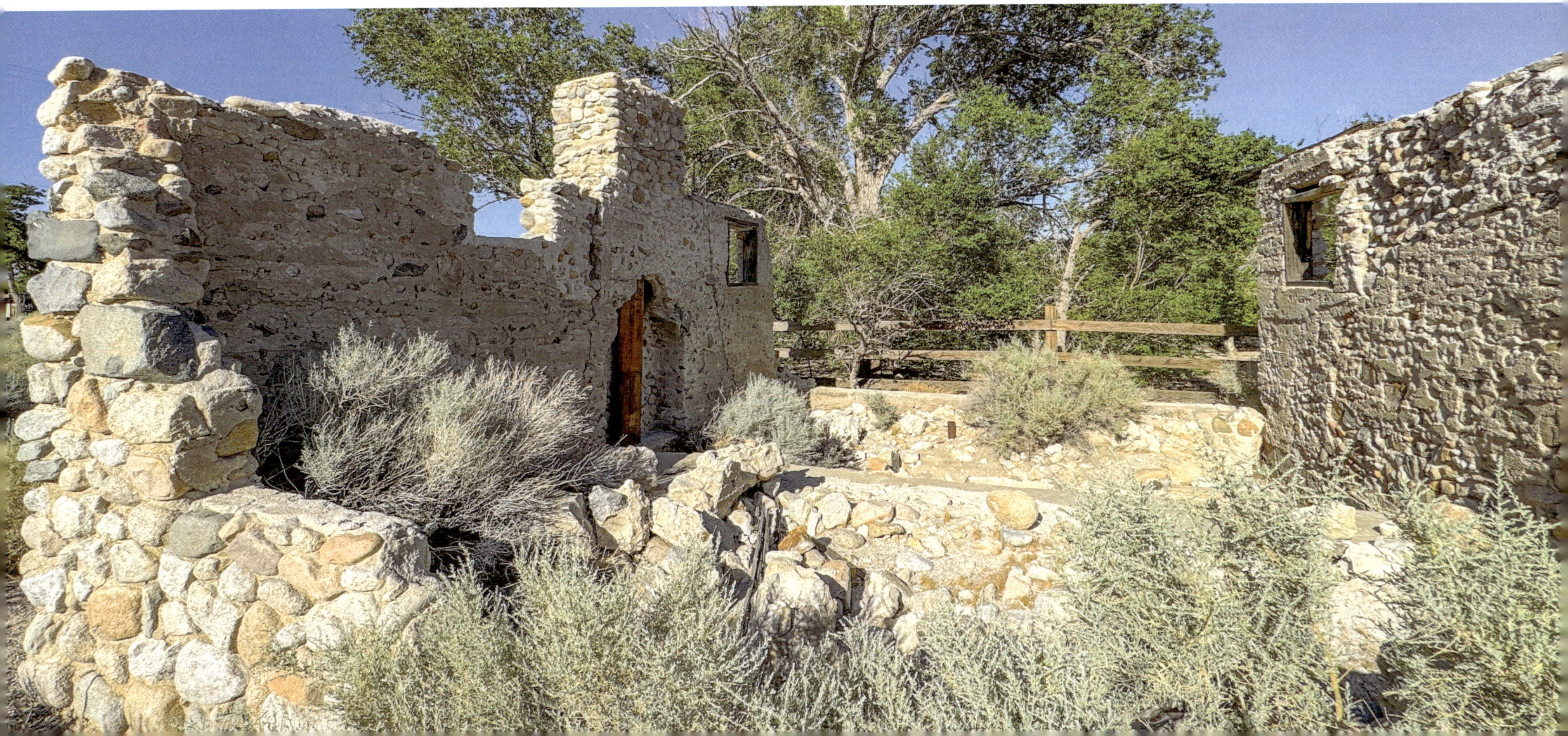

# DUNMOVIN

James Cowan opened Cowan Station in the early 1900s to serve freighters and miners from Cerro Gordo. With the arrival of the Roosevelt Midland Trail, the station moved a short distance to the new automobile road. Cowan's became a combination service station, store, hotel, and restaurant until it closed during the Great Depression.

Charles and Hilda King purchased Cowan Station in 1936. They had relocated multiple times, and deciding this was their last move, they renamed the town Dunmovin.

Following the Kings' deaths, the station changed hands several times, and a small town grew around it. Dunmovin remained a travel center until the 1970s.

GRINDING STONE

# LITTLE LAKE

The settlement on Little Lake was a waystation on the road between Keeler, Cerro Gordo, and Mojave. Travelers rested, fished, and hunted ducks. A post office opened in 1909 but lasted only two years.

In February 1909, the Southern Pacific created a station south of Little Lake to facilitate the construction of the Los Angeles Aqueduct. It was named Narka, and a post office opened that spring. The Narka post office transferred to Little Lake in June 1913. The following year, the William Bramlette family purchased the property. In 1919, they started the construction of a new hotel, which took four years to complete.

In 1954, the Matheny family purchased Little Lake and updated the hotel, swimming pool, gift shop, and neon sign. Little Lake was the first postcard ever printed in color. Little Lake continued to serve travelers with fuel, food, and supplies.

Highway 395 was realigned in 1958, bypassing Little Lake. Southern Pacific abandoned their line in 1981. Sadly, a fire destroyed the hotel in 1989. A decade later, the remaining structures were demolished; only the post office was spared.

# CLAIR CAMP

In 1896, Henry Ratcliff began working the Never Give Up Mine, and the Montgomery brothers worked the World Beater Mine.

The mines employed 200 men combined. The mining camp that developed included a blacksmith, assay office, and businesses. The mines worked to create a post office on the flats below the mining camp. The camp could not support the number of residents, leading to the settlement of Ballarat.

In five years, $500,000 ($19 million in 2025) in gold was extracted from the mines. However, mining strikes at Skidoo and Tonopah, Nevada, caused miners to abandon the mines.

W.D. Clair purchased the Ratcliff in 1930, and the settlement became known as Clair Camp. He worked the old tailings, extracting $60,000 in gold ($1.1 million in 2025).

After serving in the Vietnam War, Rodney Lane was discharged from the Marine Corps. Looking for solitude, he and his wife, Carol, camped at Clair Camp. Lane made a deal with the Clair family to live at their camp and pay a small amount of rent in return for looking over the property.

In May 1971, the couple and their infant daughter set out for their new home in a pickup truck. The truck was loaded with 300 pounds of supplies: a dog, five cats, five goats, and two burros. The Lane family only made it as far as Ballarat before it became apparent the road was in no condition for the heavily burdened truck. Undeterred, they strapped supplies on the burros, Jennie and Lupe, and headed up the canyon. Lupe the burro had special cargo: baby Jennifer strapped in a specially made pouch. The swaying of the burro acted as a rocker, and Jennifer slept the entire six-and-a-half-mile hike to Clair Camp.

# BALLARAT

Ballarat was born in 1897 to support the mines of Pleasant Canyon (which later came to be known as Clair Camp). The camp was named after Ballarat, Australia, the site of that country's first gold strike.

From 1897 to 1905, over 500 people called Ballarat home, and it became a supply and entertainment center for the mining region. The town consisted of hotels, restaurants, a post office, a school, and a jail for those who got too rowdy at its seven saloons. The one thing Ballarat lacked was a church.

The town declined in the early 1900s as mining decreased. In 1917, the postal service closed the Ballarat post office.

A handful of Old West characters remained over the years. The famous Death Valley prospector "Shorty Harris," who referred to himself as a "single blanket-jackass prospector," lived in Ballarat sporadically until he died in 1934. Charles Ferge, better known as "Seldom Seen Slim," remained in Ballarat until his death. Due to lack of water, he hadn't bathed in two decades. He is buried in the Ballarat Cemetery, "where the digging's easy."

In the 21st century, a handful call Ballarat home. The store is a popular meeting place for off-road groups; you can purchase water, snacks, and a "Ballarat Smart-Ass" t-shirt.

# REILLY

The Wibbett brothers discovered silver ore in 1875. In the spring of 1882, Edward Reilly from New York purchased the claims. He organized the Argus Range Silver and Mining Company with $500,000 in stock ($16 million in 2025).

Sixty workers leveled the site for a ten-stamp mill. Charles Anthony built and ran the hotel, barns, and blacksmith shop. Reilly built his home northwest of the ravine while the boarding house was on the south end. A pipeline brought water five miles from Water Canyon. Water to the mill was enough to power thirty stamps.

A post office opened on January 22, 1883. It closed only nine months later, on October 15, 1883, just as the mill began production.

The ore from Reilly's mines was rich but lacking in quantity. Reilly's mill processed ore from George Hearst's claims. The mines were worked periodically into the early 1900s when an arrastra was created. Reilly produced $21,500 ($785,000 in 2025), only 10% of the initial $200,000 investment ($6.3 million in 2025).

THE MANSION

# DUBLIN GULCH

Miners and railroad workers constructed cabins using what supplies were available. Most were built with stone, and the fortunate few used lumber or railroad ties. At Dubin Gulch, they used a large bluff of volcanic ash, digging cave dwellings into the cliffside.

The caves remained cool in the summer and warm on cold Mojave winter nights. Most homes were single-roomed, but some had multiple rooms and even a garage. Fireplaces vented through a stove pipe through the top of the bluff. Shorty Harris and the Ashford Brothers were well-known people who once called Dublin Gulch home.

As one resident moved or died, others jockeyed for the more desirable caves. The lucky few lived in "The Mansion," with an ornate oak door from Rhyolite.

In 1953, Dublin Gulch resident Shorty O'Bannon witnessed a drunk woman shoot her husband in Shoshone. He drove home to report the crime, crashing his car due to his intoxication. The constable arrested Shorty, but he saved the shooting victim's life.

"Papa Jim" Standing was Dublin Gulch's last resident. He moved into the Ashfords' cave following their death and lived there until the 1970s.

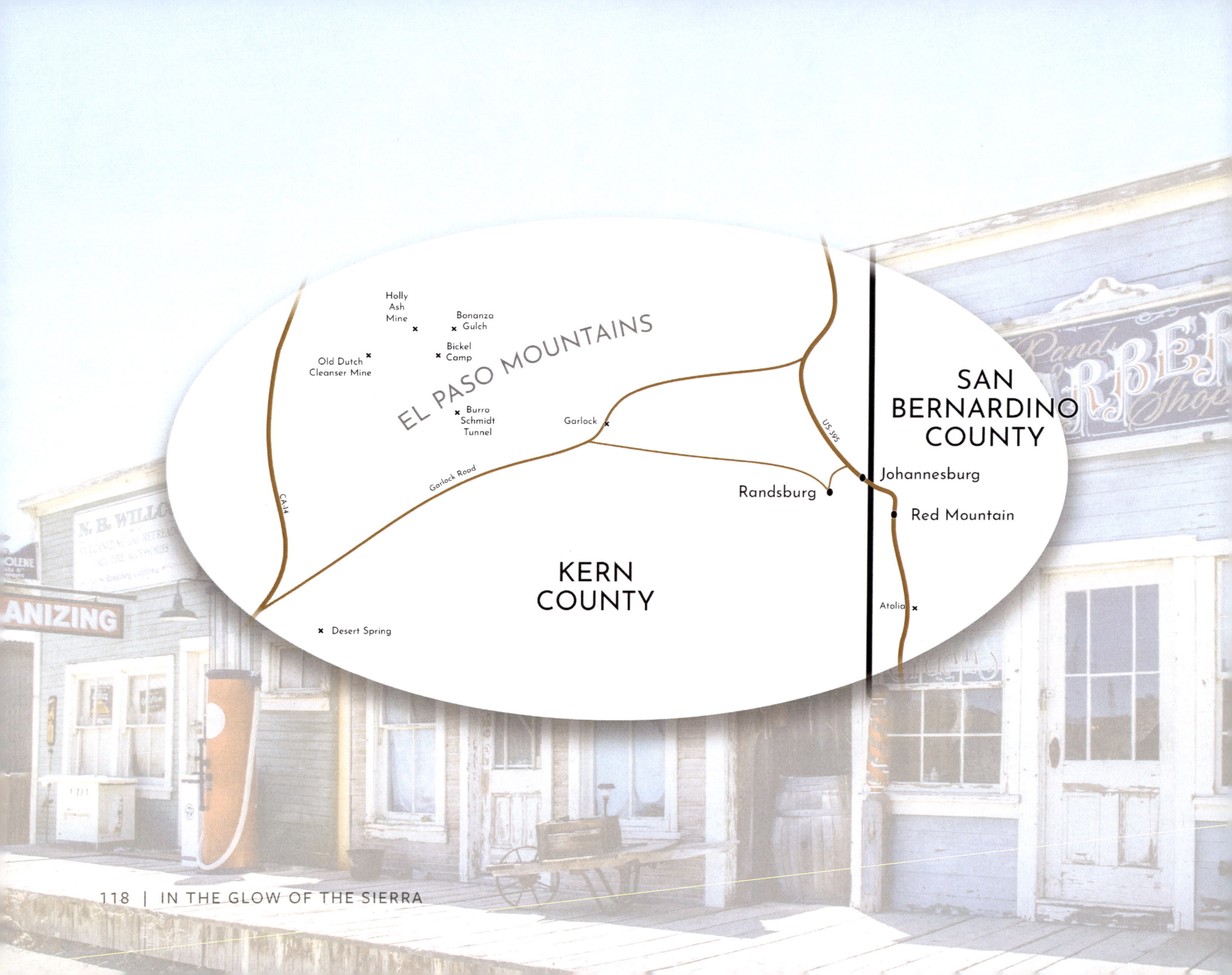

Holly
Ash
Mine ✕

Bonanza
✕ Gulch

Old Dutch ✕
Cleanser Mine

Bickel
✕ Camp

EL PASO MOUNTAINS

✕ Burro
Schmidt
Tunnel

Garlock ✕

SAN
BERNARDINO
COUNTY

US 395

Garlock Road

Johannesburg

Randsburg •

CA-14

Red Mountain

KERN
COUNTY

Atolia ✕

✕ Desert Spring

# *Chapter Three:* KERN AND SAN BERNARDINO COUNTIES

**The Old Spanish Trail was a trade route between Santa Fe, New Mexico, and Los Angeles, California, used from the 1830s to the 1850s. At 700 miles long, it was considered one of the most challenging trade routes in the United States.**

Following the disasters the Donner Party faced, others looked for alternatives to cross the Sierra. Arriving in Salt Lake City late in 1849, the Manly-Jayhawk Party opted for the southern tip of the Sierra, traversable in winter. The party faced multiple issues and split several times. While trying to avoid the fate of freezing to death and cannibalism, the "Lost '49ers" left the Spanish Trail, thinking to cut 500 miles off their route. Sadly, their journey was as disastrous as the Donner Party, with many dying of thirst and hunger, leading to the naming of Death Valley.

Following the end of the Gold Rush, mining and settlement in California declined. Wanting to encourage the settlement of the western United States, the US government passed several acts, including the Homestead Act of 1862, the General Mining Act of 1872, and the Desert Land Act of 1877. These acts allowed citizens and intended citizens to claim 160 to 640 acres of public lands for farming, ranching, and mining.

Wagon roads followed the few precious natural springs in the Mojave Desert, and stations soon developed. Prospectors spread out among the hills. Stations added arrastras and stamp mills to process ore from the mines. In 1893, a $1,900 ($68,000 in 2025) gold nugget was found at Goler Heights, starting the mining rush. Two years later, partners founded the famous Yellow Aster Mine, which produced $600,000 in gold ($22 million in 2025).

With the onset of World War I and World War II, mining in the Southern and Eastern Sierras was revived to support the war effort, and it was revived later for various household products.

# OLD DUTCH CLEANSER
# & HOLLY ASH MINES

From 1923 to 1947, the Old Dutch Cleanser Company mined pumice for cleaning products. Twelve men produced 100 tons of pumice a week. Burros hauled the pumice slabs to the aerial tram, which lowered them to the valley below. They were then hauled to the Southern Pacific Railroad at Saltdale. During the Great Depression, miners from Mexico worked the Old Dutch Cleanser Mine for less pay than local miners were willing to accept.

The Old Dutch Cleanser Mine produced 120,000 tons of pumice in its twenty-four years of operation.

The Holly Ash Mine was first worked in 1919. The pumice was used in cleaning products, including Holly Cleanser. The pumice was pulverized into ash, then bagged on site and transported to Los Angeles via truck or rail.

In 1946, the Calsilco Corporation assumed control of the Holly Ash. The ash was sold as a painkiller and oil-absorbing compound.

# BICKEL CAMP

Walter Bickel had always been inventive. As a teen, he built a racecar from junk vehicles. He even built an aircraft engine powerful enough to blow out his father's barn walls.

Bickel first visited the El Paso Mountains in 1927. He returned in 1934, building a cabin in Last Chance Canyon. To support his family, he owned a business in Los Angeles, which he lost in the Great Depression. He worked several jobs, spending weekends at his cabin.

Bickel enlisted in the army in 1942. He noticed crews having difficulty changing hot machine gun barrels. He received a medal for developing a tool that allowed soldiers to change the barrels in combat.

Following World War II, Bickel returned to his mine. Living in his cabin, he added a trailer for his wife and children. Bickel helped fellow miners dig wells and repair equipment, often accepting barter for payment. He helped stranded motorists, welcoming them into his cabin for home-cooked meals.

In the 1980s, the Bureau of Land Management developed a plan to prevent squatters from living in the desert by knocking down cabins. Many mining claims were deemed too small to warrant a structure on site. Hours before the arrival of BLM inspectors, Bickel had a stroke, requiring him to live in a nursing home. His family and friends banded together to save Bickel Camp. Working with the BLM, they preserved his camp, creating an open-air museum. A curator is on site during the weekends to welcome visitors.

# BONANZA GULCH

Following the tragedy of the Donner Party in 1846 to 1847, emigrants searched for alternate routes across the Sierra. In the fall of 1849, a group of wagons was organized in Salt Lake City. It was too late in the season to cross the treacherous range, and not wanting to remain in Utah, they searched for alternate routes.

One hundred and seven wagons set out for the Spanish Trail. The more established route went around the southern end of the Sierra and could be traveled over winter. The wagon party split with twenty men, including John Goler, continuing on the route through what is now Death Valley.

Having seen gold on the treacherous journey, Goler returned to search for the canyon. Goler never did find his Atlantis, but word spread, and soon, miners were combing the El Paso Mountains.

Over one hundred years, prospectors staked claims and built cabins to watch over their mine and equipment. In the 1980s, squatters became an issue in the desert. The Bureau of Land Management developed a plan to reduce squatters and remove many old cabins. A few survived as part of the BLM "Adopt a Cabin" program. Non-profit groups adopted the old mining cabins, preserving them for visitors who can stay in them on a first-come, first serve basis.

# BURRO SCHMIDT TUNNEL

Not wanting to haul the ore from his mine over a dangerous ridge, William "Burro" Schmidt dug a tunnel through the El Paso Mountains. He initially dug the tunnel by hand. Later, he used dynamite with a "notoriously short fuse" to blast through the hard granite. The tunnel was six feet tall and ten feet wide. The tunnel required little shoring, but Burro was trapped multiple times in collapses. He transported much of the rock in a wheelbarrow, eventually adding rails and a mining cart.

Burro supported his dream by working as a ranch hand in the summers. Each fall, he returned to his obsession with his burros, Jack and Jenny.

In 1920, a road was built connecting Last Chance Canyon to Mojave. Undeterred, Burro continued working on his tunnel. For thirty-eight years, he worked underground, earning him the name "The Human Mole" from *Ripley's Believe It or Not*.

Burro completed his tunnel in 1936. He never transported ore through it but partnered with Mike Lee to give tours of the tunnel.

Evelyn Tonie Seger and her husband purchased Burro's cabin and mines after he and Lee died in 1954 and 1963, respectively. Evelyn continued to live at the cabin after her husband's death. She was a tough woman, fighting off claim jumpers. The final straw was when a claim jumper showed up armed. She knocked the revolver from his hand, saying if he came back again, he'd better be prepared to use it. Evelyn lived at the mine until she died in 2003 at age ninety-eight. Evelyn is buried alongside Burro at the Johannesburg cemetery.

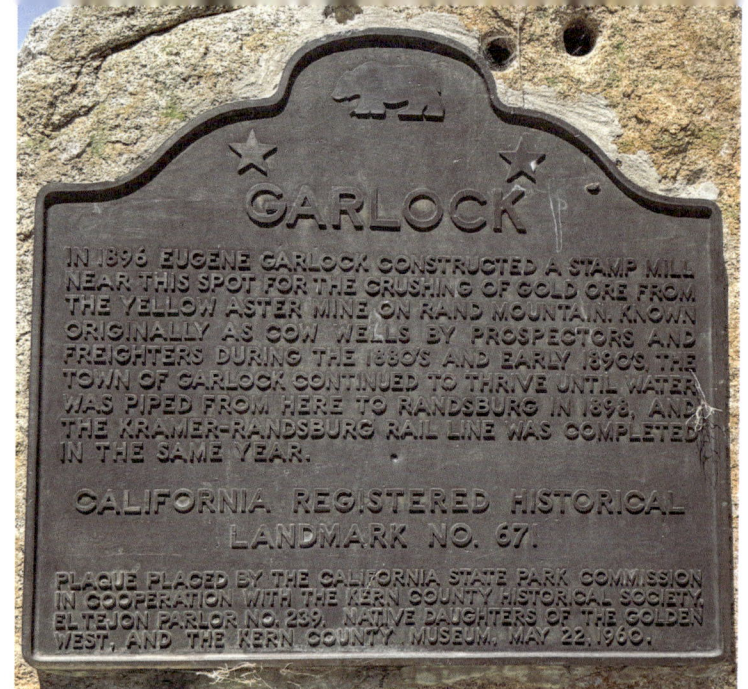

# GARLOCK

Initially called Cow Wells, then El Paso City, the spring was used by cattlemen as a watering hole along their route. An enterprising woman set up a store and restaurant in a single-room shack. The isolated location and primitive town of one hundred was known as the closest bastion of civilization for the miners exploring the El Paso Mountains.

Mining was productive enough to warrant the building of an arrastra in 1887. Prospectors crushed their ore in this primitive mill. Drag stones suspended from an arm made continuous circles in the arrastra powered by humans, burros, or steam.

In 1893, a $1,900 ($68,000 in 2025) gold nugget was found at Goler Heights, starting the district's mining rush. Eugene Garlock built the Garlock Pioneer Mill, an eight-stamp mill to process ore from the Yellow Aster Mine in El Paso Mountain. Five more mills joined Garlock's.

The settlement grew into a full-fledged town with a population of 600, including only sixteen women. A post office opened in 1896, along with a school and church. Garlock soon had every service imaginable, including stores, boarding houses, barbers, and a physician. The Garlock Literary Society met at the church, giving the town a moral compass.

The saloons, including Cheney's Thirst Emporium, were the most popular businesses in Garlock. At least one saloon had a gambling hall and cribs for prostitutes. To guard against prohibitionists, the saloons formed their security force, the Wirecutter's Association.

Garlock thrived until 1898, when water was diverted to Randsburg, spelling the end for Garlock.

# JOHANNESBURG

The tent town of Johannesburg grew to support the Rand Mining District, selecting a name to keep with the district's South African theme. Soon, organizers planned a higher-class, family-oriented town with grid streets. The town grew to include a post office, various stores, boarding houses, a music hall, and a pool hall. The Johannesburg Jack Rabbit Golf Course opened in the 1890s, one of California's first golf courses.

Johannesburg mining companies dug the region's first wells. Primitive mills, or arrastras, processed the region's ore until stamp mills opened.

The Randbsurg Railway was completed in 1898. It connected Johannesburg to the Atchison, Topeka, and Santa Fe Railroad at Kramer Junction.

The Rand District Community Cemetery started in 1896 with the burial of William Davis, who was shot and killed in Randsburg over a gambling dispute. It is the only cemetery in the region; many early pioneers and miners are buried here, including William "Burro" Schmidt.

A telegraph connected Johannesburg to Mojave, and a telephone line connected to the nearby sister city of Randsburg. The telephone was a party line, meaning others could listen to conversations. Couples in the towns used the phone to court, sometimes forgetting the lack of privacy. The *Randsburg Miner* newspaper was happy for fodder and printed conversations about "who had been making love to whom over the phone."

# RANDSBURG

In 1894, Frederic Mooers and William Langdon prospected the Red Mountain Range and found small amounts of gold. The following year, Mooers returned with Charles Burcham and John Singleton and discovered a rich gold vein. The trio devised a scheme to protect their discovery until they filed a legal claim to their mine. They loaded sacks of worthless iron-stained quartz, rode back to the camp at Goler, and announced they had made a discovery. Leaving the sack unattended, veteran miners inspected their "discovery" only to find the worthless rock. Believing the partners were inexperienced and clueless, the other miners continued their prospecting.

Charles Burcham and his wife, Dr. Rose Burcham, secured a mining claim in 1895. Rose advised her husband not to sell their claim until they knew its worth. Mooers and Langdon wanted to sell their claim, but Burcham remembered his wife's advice and refused to sign.

The partners formed the Yellow Aster Mine, one of the few mines to be developed by the founders. Dr. Rose Burcham was a rare woman for her time. In 1895, she left her medical practice and moved to Rand Camp in the Mojave Desert. She headed the Yellow Aster Mine, becoming the manager, bookkeeper, and secretary.

Rand Camp grew to support the mines. In 1896, with a population of 1,500, the town changed its name to Randsburg and opened a post office. The following year, 2,500 souls called Randsburg home, and the town had over 300 buildings. On January 19, 1897, half of Randsburg was destroyed by fire. The town was soon rebuilt, and Randsburg grew to include over 3,500 people by 1899.

Randsburg was a typical mining town with twenty-four saloons, brothels, and gunfights over gambling disputes. The *Randsburg Newspaper* reported, "What this town needs is more water and less whiskey."

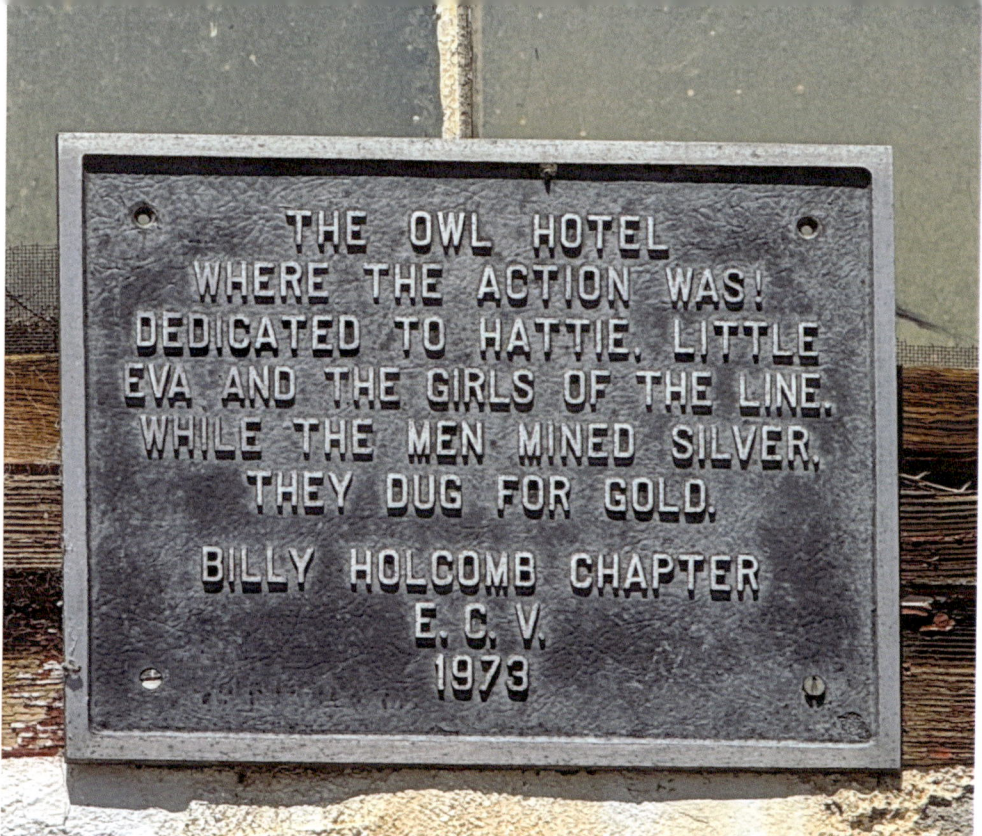

# RED MOUNTAIN

Jack Nosser and W. H. Williams discovered silver ore on April 12, 1919. Lacking funds to develop the mine, they partnered with the sheriff of Kern County, John Kelly, and his friends. The ore was so rich and shallow that they extracted $1.7 million ($32 million in 2025) of silver in the first two months. The Kelly Silver Mine became the nation's largest producer of silver. It was so pure that it was considered "horn-silver" and required no processing. Despite the devaluation of silver, the Kelly Mine continued to operate, producing an astounding $13,000,000 ($241 million in 2025).

In 1919, the town of Osdick grew to support the mine. A post office opened in 1922, and the town later changed its name to Red Mountain. One of the town's first saloons was

The Northern, which opened in 1919. In the 1930s, the name was changed to the Silver Dollar Saloon.

During prohibition, Red Mountain was a "wide-open town." Visitors came far and wide to enjoy drinking, gambling, and brothels. Saloons, gambling halls, and houses of ill repute lined the main street. The Owl Hotel was said to be "where the action was!" and "While the men mined silver, they (prostitutes) dug for gold."

# ATOLIA

Atolia grew to support tungsten mining. It was named after Atkins and DeGolia, two mining company executives. A post office opened in 1906, and Atolia grew to a population of 2,000. The town included four restaurants, three stores, boarding houses, a movie theater, a dairy, and the Bucket of Blood Saloon.

With the start of World War I, tungsten was in high demand as it was used to harden steel alloys. Atolia became the primary source of tungsten in the world.

Before the United States entered WWI, Germany was the largest purchaser of Atolia's tungsten. However, the English naval blockade prevented German cargo ships from reaching the United States. Germany created the first cargo submarine, the U-boat, to avoid the blockades.

On July 9, 1916, the German submarine *Deutschland* docked in Baltimore. Among the cargo were hundreds of sacks of tungsten concentrate from Atolia, which had been shipped under armed guard on the Randsburg Railway.

With the end of WWI, demand for tungsten declined, and the mines closed. Residents moved on, and the post office closed in 1922. Atolia's mines reopened with the onset of WWII and continued into the 1960s, but the town never returned to its former glory.

# DESERT SPRING

Native Americans first used the freshwater at Desert Spring. Famed explorers Joseph Walker and John Frémont visited the spring in 1834 and 1844, respectively.

Desert Spring was a stopping place as early as the 1830s on the Indian Horsethief Trail, part of the Old Spanish Trail. The Manly-Jawhawk party recuperated at Desert Spring after their harrowing escape from Death Valley.

Between 1869 and 1882, Remi Nadeau was the "king of mule-wagon freighting." His Cerro Gordo Freighting Company traversed the 230-mile Nadeau Road connecting Cerro Gordo to San Pedro, California. The line had eighty wagons, each able to carry four tons, the same as a narrow-gauge railcar. Each wagon had sixteen to twenty-two mules, and the round-trip took twenty-two days. The freighters stopped at multiple watering holes and stations, including Desert Spring.

# REFERENCES

## BOOKS

Basso, Dave. *Nevada Historical Marker Guidebook*. Nevada Publications, 1986. Page 166.

Browning, Peter. *Place Names of the Sierra Nevada*. Wilderness Press, 1986.

Cain, Ella M. *The Story of Bodie*. Fearon Publishers, 1956.

California Bureau of Mines. *Mines of Alpine, Inyo and Mono Counties*, California. 1917.

Canton, Wanda and Richard. *Bodie Railway and Lumber Company: Railroad in the Sky 1881-1917*. Friends of Bodie Railway and Lumber Company, Inc. 2011.

Carlson, Helen S. *Nevada Place Names: A Geographical Dictionary*. University of Nevada Press, 1974.

Carson Valley Historical Society. *Snowshoe Thompson*. 1991.

Chalfant, Willie Arthur. *The Story of Inyo*. Hammond Press, 1922.

Dangberg, Grace. *Conflict on the Carson*. Carson Valley Historical Society, 1975.

DeDecker, Mary. *Mines of the Eastern Sierra*. La Siesta Press, 1993.

Desmarais, Robert. *Cero Gordo: My life in the ghost town*. 2023.

Dustman, Karen. *Historic Alpine: A Driving Tour of Woodfords, Diamond Valley & Fredericksburg Historic Sites*. Clairitage Press, 2019.

Dustman, Karen. *Markleeville: A Walking Tour*. Clairitage Press, 2014.

Dustman, Karen. *Silver Mountain City*. Clairitage Press, 2011.

Ellison, Robert W. *First Impressions: The trail through Carson Valley 1848-1852*. Hot Springs Mountain Press, 2001.

Fey, Marshall. *Emigrant Trails: The Long Road to California, A history and Guide to the Emigrant Routes from Central Nevada to Crossing the Sierra*. Nevada Publication, 2019.

Gamett, James and Stan Paher. *Nevada Post Offices: An Illustrated History*. Nevada Publications, 1863. Page 134.

Gudde, Erwin G. California Gold Camps: *A geographical dictionary of camps, towns, and localities where gold was found and Mined: Wayside Stations and Trading Centers*. University of California Press, 1975.

Hastings, Lansford W. *The 1845 Pioneers' Guide for the Westward Traveler: The Emigrants' Guide to Oregon and California*. Applewood Books, 1845.

Huegel, Tony. *Sierra Nevada Byways: 51 of the Sierra Nevada's Best Backcountry Drives*. Wilderness Press, 2008.

Irwin, Catherine. *Twice Orphaned: Voices from the Children's Village of Manzanar*. California State University Fullerton, 2008.

*Journal of the Modoc County Historical Society*. Volume 4. 1982.

Lincoln, Francis Church. *Mining Districts and Mineral Resources of Nevada*. Nevada Publications, 1982.

Lingenfelter, Richard E and Karen Rix Gash. *The Newspapers of Nevada: A history and bibliography 1854-1979* T. University of Nevada Press, 1984.

Makley, Michael J. *Imposing Order without Law: American expansion to the Eastern Sierra 1850-1865*. University of Nevada Press, 2022.

Massey et al. *California Trails: High Sierra Region*. Adler Publishing, 2006.

McGlashan, C.F. *History of the Donner Party*. Press of the City Printing Company, 1939.

McGrath, Roger D. *Gunfighters, Highway Men and Vigilantes: Violence on the Frontier*. University of California Press, 1894.

Mitchell, Roger. *High Sierra SUV Trails, Volume 1, The East Side*. Track and Trail Publications, 2002.

Mitchell, Roger. *Inyo-Mono SUV Trails*. Track and Trail Publications, 2003.

Miluck, Nancy C. *Nevada This is our Land: A survey from Prehistory to Present*. Dragon Enterprises, 1994.

Murbarger, Nell. *Ghosts of the Glory Trail*. Westernlore Press, 1956.

Myrick, David F. *Railroads of Nevada and Eastern California Volumes I, II, III*. University of Nevada Press. 1990, 1991, 2007.

Nation, Nyle. *The Pine Nut Chronicle: The History and Adventures of Mining in Douglas County, Nevada*. Pine Nut Press, 2000.

Newton, Marilyn. *Alkali Angels: Recording Nevada's Historic Graveyards*. Carmel Publishing Company, 2004. Page 174.

Nevada Historical Society Quarterly

Paher, Stanley W. *Death Valley Ghost Towns Volume 1*. Nevada Press. 1973.

Paher, Stanley W. *Death Valley Ghost Towns Volume 2*. Nevada Press. 1981.

Paher, Stanley. *Nevada Ghost Towns and Mining Camps*. Nevada Publications, 1970.

Paher, Stanley. *Nevada Ghost Towns & Desert Atlas*, Nevada Press 2020.

Patera, Alan H. and David A. Wright. *Skidoo: Including Harrisburg and Emigrant Springs*. Western Places, 1999.

Raty, Mary Sauer. *Pioneers of the Ponderosa: How Washoe Vallay rescued the Comstock*. Western Printing and Publishing Company. 1973.

Reiser, Marc. *Cadillac Desert: The American west and its disappearing water*. Viking Penguin, 1986.

Riddle, Jennifer E., Sena M. Loyd, Stacy L. Branham, and Curt Thomas. *Images of America: Nevada State Prison*. Arcadia Publishing, 2012.

Salley, H.E. *History of California Post Offices 1849-1976*. Heartland Printing and Publishing Company. 1977

Shamberger, Hugh. *The story of the water supply for the Comstock*. United States Department of the Interior. 1972.

Silver, Sue. *Aurora Nevada's Silent City on the Hill*. Museum Associates of Mineral County, 2011.

Silver, Sue. *Along the East Walker River: An historical perspective*. 2013.

Silver, Sue. Volume 1. *Mineral County Nevada: Mining Camps, Towns, & Places (1860-1900)*, 2011.

Silver, Sue. *Mineral County Nevada: Volume 2, Mining Camps, Towns, & Places (901 and after)*, 2011.

Silver, Sue. *Volume 3: Mineral County, Nevada: Volume, Early Transportation, Stagecoach, Steamboat and Narrow Gauge Rail*. Museum Associates of Mineral County, 2011.

Silver, Sue. *Volume 4: Progress and People*. Museum Associates of Mineral County, 2011.

Silver, Sue. *Volume 5: Mineral County, Nevada: Roads and Routes of the Past*. Museum Associates of Mineral County, 2012.

Silver, Sue. *Mineral County, Nevada: Volume 5, Roads and Routes of the Past*. Museum Associates of Mineral County, 2012.

Somerville, June Wood. *A Legend of a Road. A witness to the exploration and emigration on the road above Silver Lake and beyond*. June Wood Somerville, 2014.

Stewart, George R. *Ordeal by Hunger: The story of the Donner Party*. Houghton Mifflin Company, 1988.

Stewart, Robert E. *Aurora: Nevada's Ghost City of the Dawn*. Nevada Publications, 2004. Pages 67-70.

Stories from Mimi: *The Water Works: Virginia City & Gold Hill*, Nevada

Smith, Grant H. *The History of the Comstock Lode*. University of Nevada Press, 1997. Page 45.

The Natural Wealth of California: Comprising Early History; Geography, Topography, and Scenery; Climate; Agriculture and Commercial Products; Geology, Zoology, and Botany; Mineralogy, Mines, and Mining Processes; Manufactures; Steamship Lines, Railroads, and Commerce; Immigration, Population and Society; Educational Institutions and Literature; Together with a Detailed Description of Each County

Tortorich, Frank Jr. *Gold Rush Trail: A guide to the Carson River Route of the Emigrant Trail*. Wagon Wheel Tours, 1998.

Tortorich, Frank. *John "Snowshoe' Thompson: Pioneer mail carrier of the Sierra*. Pronghornpress, 2015.

Underwood, Brent. *Ghost Town Living: Mining for purpose and chasing dreams at the edge of Death Valley.* 2024.

Wakatskui Houston, Jeanne & James D. Houston. *Farwell to Manzanar.* Dell Laurel-Leaf. 1973.

Wedertz, Frank S. Mono Diggings. *Historical Sketches of Old Bridgeport Big Meadows and Vicinity.* Chalfant Press, 1978.

## NEWSPAPERS

*Indian Valley Record, March 2, 1939*

The Daily Appeal Dec 4, 1900: December Hay Making

*Mono Herald and Bridgeport Chronicle-Union July 21, 1906 Found Dead at Dogtown*

*The Daily Appeal, June 1, 1893 War at Buckeye*

*The Silver State, June 2, 1893 Fight over a mine*

*The Daily Appeal, June 18, 1893 Stevenson---Raycraft*

The Oregonian March 10, 1911 Snowslides Deals Death on Heights

*Reno Gazette-Journal*

Weekly Nevada State Journal, May 19, 1877

The White Pine News, August 16, 1884

*Los Angeles Times, December 11, 1950 Opened in 1860s*

*Mono Herald and Bridgeport Chronicle-Union* Mammoth Lakes, California · Saturday, January 31, 1891 A rich silver strike

*Mono Herald and Bridgeport Chronicle-Union* Mammoth Lakes, California · Saturday, June 12, 1909 Sweetwater

*The Peninsula Times Tribune* Palo Alto, California · Monday, March 20, 1939 Jim Townsend Publisher

*Yerington Times* Yerington, Nevada ● Sat, Aug 25, 1917 *Silverado Canyon*

*Silverado Mine Yerington Times, December 29, 1926*

*Famed mine reactivated Los Angeles Times, December 11, 1950*

*Burke and Cockerell Gold Hill Daily News October 24, 1871* February 8, 1924

*Prospects in Mono San Francisco Chronicle* San Francisco, California · Thursday, June 04, 1885

*The Ventura Free Press* Ventura, California · Saturday, December 16, 1876

Dispute about a mine *The San Francisco Examiner* San Francisco, California · Tuesday, January 07, 1896

*Mono Herald and Bridgeport Chronicle-Union* Mammoth Lakes, California · Thursday, June 14, 1979

*Mono Herald and Bridgeport Chronicle-Union* Mammoth Lakes, California · Thursday, August 19, 1982

Old Mine Regino in Mono County is coming back *Oakland Tribune* Oakland, California · Tuesday, July 21, 1925

Good Outlook for mining *Mono Herald and Bridgeport Chronicle-Union* Mammoth Lakes, California · Wednesday, November 24, 1920

Our Camp in 1864 Mono Herald and Bridgeport Chronicle-Union September 16, 1976

Riches in Mono *Walker Lake Bulletin* Hawthorne, Nevada · Wednesday, November 07, 1883

The Sacramento Mine *Yerington Times* Yerington, Nevada · Saturday, May 19, 1883

*Mono Herald and Bridgeport Chronicle-Union* Mammoth Lakes, California · Saturday, October 20, 1883

Inyo Items *Walker Lake Bulletin* Hawthorne, Nevada · Wednesday, November 07, 1883

White Mountain

*Mono Herald and Bridgeport Chronicle-Union* Mammoth Lakes, California · Thursday, December 29, 1938

*Mono Herald and Bridgeport Chronicle-Union* Mammoth Lakes, California · Friday, October 08, 1965

*Mono Herald and Bridgeport Chronicle-Union* Mammoth Lakes, California · Friday, February 04, 1966 Company at Work *Mono Herald and Bridgeport Chronicle-Union* Mammoth Lakes, California · Saturday, March 02, 1912

Indian Title to Land Simple one in early years The San Bernardino County Sun San Bernardino, California · Sunday, February 02, 1958

The San Francisco Examiner: Gold But How much? San Francisco, California Thu, Aug 13, 1891 · Page 1

Los Angeles Times, December 11, 1950

Mason Valley News, March 24, 1961

Mono Herald and Bridgeport Chronicle-Union, January 31, 1891

Mono Herald and Bridgeport Chronicle-Union, June 12, 1909

Yerington Times, August 25, 1917

Mono Herald and Bridgeport Chronicle Union, January 5, 1918

Herald and Bridgeport Chronicle Union January 30, 1941

Reno Gazette-Journal April 12, 1883

Reno Gazette-Journal, July 15, 1938

Reno Gazette-Journal August 13, 1942

The Salt Lake Tribune, June 5, 1936

Western Mining History: Silverado Mine

Yerington Times, November 17, 1926

Yerington Times, December 29, 1926

D.Q.C. (*March 28, 1864*). *"Letter from Mono County".* *Sacramento Daily Union.*

Report of Testimony taken before the Committee on Elections of the Senate, in the contested Election Case of Cavis vs. Quint" ; "Report of Assembly Committee on Elections relative to the contested Election Case of Orr vs. Davis."; Items 37 and 39 in *Appendix to Journals of Senate and Assembly, Thirteenth Session of the Legislature of the State of California.* Sacramento: Benj. P. Avery, State Printer 1862.

*Other Interview with Barbra Byington*

## WEBSITES

Bureau of Land Management https://www.blm.gov

Clairitage Press https://www.clairitage.com

David Rumsey map Collection https://www.davidrumsey.com/luna/servlet/RUMSEY~8~1

Dennis Cassinelli: https://denniscassinelli.com

California Office of Historic Preservation https://ohp.parks.ca.gov

Donner Summit Historical Society https://www.donnersummithistoricalsociety.org/pages/petroglyphs.html

Exploring Lassen Counties Past https://www.citlink.net/~lahontan/susanville.htm

Great Basin Institute: Tallac Historic Site https://taylortallac.org/tallac-historic-site-home/

The Inn at Benton Hot Springs https://www.bentonhotsprings.us/

Lassen County Historical Society https://susanvillehistory.com

Legends of America: https://www.legendsofamerica.com

National Park Service https://www.nps.gov/index.htm

National Pony Express Association https://nationalponyexpress.org

Nevada Expeditions https://www.nvexpeditions.com/index.php

Nevada State Historical Society https://www.nvhistoricalsociety.org

Nevada State Library and Archives http://dmla.clan.lib.nv.us/docs/nsla/

Smithsonian Magazine https://www.smithsonianmag.com

University of Nevada Libraries https://library.unr.edu

Stewart Indian School https://stewartindianschool.com

US Forest Service: https://www.fs.usda.gov/recarea/ltbmu/recarea/?recid=11784
USGS https://www.usgs.gov

# INDEX

# AFTERWORD

I invite you to enjoy the rich heritage and beauty of the Eastern Sierra. Take only photographs and leave only footprints to preserve our historical resources. Please respect private property and our state and national lands. Various laws protect historical sites. Removing or damaging artifacts is illegal under federal and state laws. See the Archaeological Resources Protection Act (ARPA) for more information.

As always, be prepared when traveling. It has been over 175 years since the first emigrants traversed and settled this isolated land. Yet, the Eastern Sierra remains rugged and remote. Rocks and trees destroy vehicle tires, as they did with pioneer wagon wheels. Water and food are always a concern, as with the Donner Party and the Lost '49ers. Early settlers' only communication with the outside world was by hand-carried paper. That remains true today; cell service is non-existent in many locations.

Some sites are remote and require high clearance, 4-wheel drive vehicles, and hiking. Others are right off the highway. Whatever you drive, you can explore history along your journey.

Please follow me to see more ghost towns and historic sites in California and Nevada. You can find me at Nevada Ghost Towns & Beyond at NVTami.com, on Facebook at NVTami, on Instagram @NVTami, and on KGFN, Radio Goldfield, which you can stream to various websites.

I present at various historical and special interest groups. To request a presentation or participation at an event, email me at Tami@NVTami.com.

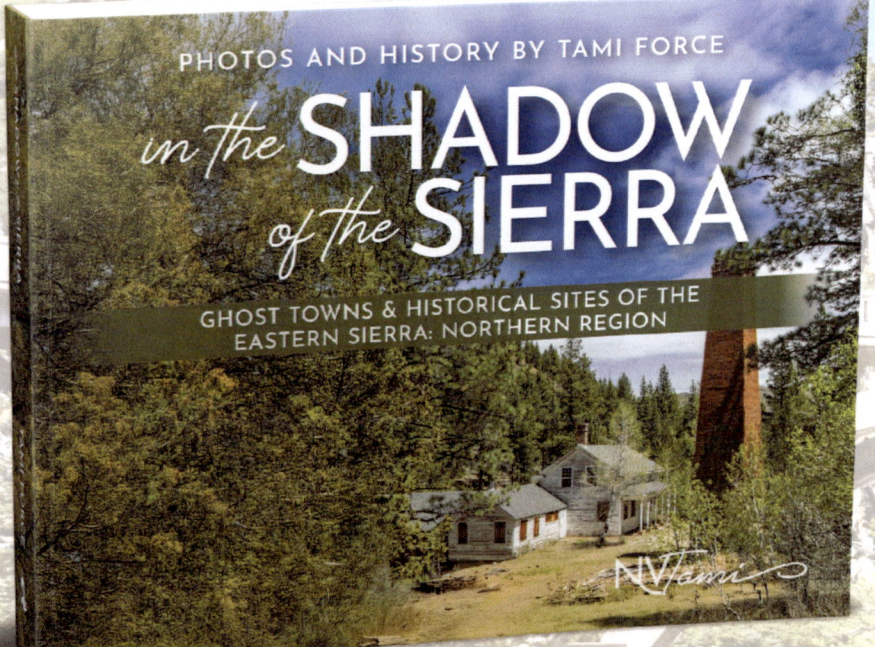

PHOTOS AND HISTORY BY TAMI FORCE

in the SHADOW of the SIERRA

GHOST TOWNS & HISTORICAL SITES OF THE
EASTERN SIERRA: NORTHERN REGION

NVTami

Continue your journey to the northern
region of the Eastern Sierra...

in the SHADOW of the SIERRA

THIS COMPANION BOOK COVERS GHOST TOWNS
AND HISTORICAL SITES FROM
LASSEN THROUGH ALPINE COUNTIES.

www.ingramcontent.com/pod-product-compliance
Lightning Source LLC
Chambersburg PA
CBRC100822120626
46551CB00010B/751